PRIMORDIAL

poems

MAI DER VANG

Graywolf Press

Published by Graywolf Press
212 Third Avenue North, Suite 485
Minneapolis, Minnesota 55401

www.graywolfpress.org

Published in the United States of America

ISBN 978-1-64445-326-1 (paperback)
ISBN 978-1-64445-327-8 (ebook)

2 4 6 8 9 7 5 3 1
First Graywolf Printing, 2025

Library of Congress Cataloging-in-Publication Data

Names: Vang, Mai Der, 1981– author.
Title: Primordial : poems / Mai Der Vang.
Description: Minneapolis, Minnesota : Graywolf Press, 2025.
Identifiers: LCCN 2024036179 (print) | LCCN 2024036180 (ebook) | ISBN 9781644453261
    (paperback) | ISBN 9781644453278 (ebook)
Subjects: LCGFT: Poetry.
Classification: LCC PS3622.A646 P75 2025 (print) | LCC PS3622.A646 (ebook) |
    DDC 811/.6—dc23/eng/20240816
LC record available at https://lccn.loc.gov/2024036179
LC ebook record available at https://lccn.loc.gov/2024036180

Cover design: Jeenee Lee

Cover art: Based on a photograph by William Robichaud / Ban Vangban Village /
    Wildlife Conservation Society

For Anthony & Máximo

For saola

CONTENTS

. . . our animals come from stars so dense in meaning close to sacrament.

—*Mei-mei Berssenbrugge*

PRIMORDIAL

Animal

We've never met   in this existence,
never scuffed   our skin   to the same

sheet of velvet.   A mirror reflects
every unopened door,   invitation

to fall through.   I've never heard you
in winter   nor have I touched my eyes

to your face.   Evening arrives
as a child   who forgets to knock,

enters without fear.   You were gone
before I could feed the wind,   left me climbing

in all directions   without   an offering
of purple corn.   I come to you

as the animal who   wants to be found,
a bowl   for a place   to fit your

nested head.   I swear not to   rush the life
where you   come back   to dream.

I'll wake and wait   all night
if that's what   the sleeping   takes.

I Arrive to Saola by Way of War

I leave the midnight to find your beginning
by way of a village weathering into ruin,
by means of men coerced into combat

by way of an empire shepherding the work
of death. I am here in California and you are
there in the Annamites. I seek you by way

of retreat, refugees fleeing a line of fire
by way of shattered twilight. High grasses
hide limbs near a cavernous sigh in the ground

by way of bombs encroaching on a footstep.
I reach the return of a people plunged into
warfare by way of proxy grab, by means of

American weapons flowing colonizer veins.
I ask you by way of foreshadows, damage
to your life is eventual damage to mine.

The torn sky in yours will rupture the bedrock
in mine. I walk the hours inside my arms to
swaddle questions by way of despair:

how does an evacuee, what of continents
apart, how do politicians away, where alongside
allies, when poaching and abandonment.

In you, a war I never encountered so much
but to be cursed. You bring me to stone dreams
of Hmong wandering foothills outside Fresno

by way of a mountain from an omitted past.
In you, cognizance of exile, shrapnel from an
American war. In you, a sequestered landscape

buried in a world searching for water
by way of every human in the conclusion
of our days. Something in you fallen diaphanous.

Something in you departed and stolen.

Relict

*. . . the new mammal belonged to the subfamily Bovinae,
which includes two great lineages of bovids: cattle, bison,
and buffalo on the one hand and spiral-horned antelope, like
gazelles, on the other.*

*Because of its facial glands and other features considered
primitive, the new animal was suspected to be a survivor of
an early bovid line that existed before cattle and antelopes
went their separate evolutionary ways.*

*. . . the new bovid was not just a new species. It also represented
a new genus, of which it was the only known member.*

—**William deBuys,** *The Last Unicorn*

I hold to you and the losses you inherited.

I hold to formation of your certainty,
grasping at the possible:

before bison and nilgai,
before anoa and nyala, before cattle and antelope,

there was you, *Pseudoryx nghetinhensis,*

mammal alive into remnant
enduring the mountains high up.

What is the creation you give yourself?

How far have you come
to seek shelter in the evergreens?

How many rebirths
in your womb's chronology?

Here into the present with a biology from the past:

maxillary glands unusually large
along the upper muzzle,

white marks on your face, tail with a stripe,
two long parallel horns.

I search my being for grace I share
with you, extent of my presence

from feet to head, incision under my belly
from where my baby emerged.

I swim my awareness alongside
pods of astral dolphins contacting
the air for seconds,

fog absorbing into sight.

Passenger of evolution, if the ancients looked
to constellations,

then I look to you,

creature who became forebear
for your kind, caretaker of the candid woods.

Animalia, immemorial.

Deduction Remains

Let's assume you've never heard of the saola.

Let's assume that if you've never heard of the saola, you
likely have never seen one either.

In your mind, it could be a gem or a tree or a kind of art.

The saola is an animal.

The saola lives in the Annamite Mountains between Laos
and Vietnam.

Though locals had long known of the saola, the animal was
first announced to the world in May 1992.

The saola was the first large mammal to be found in more
than fifty years by the Western world.

The saola belongs to the Bovidae family. Bovids are animals
with hooves and horns that include bison, buffalo, sheep,
antelope, cattle, to list a few.

The saola was determined to be a new species of Bovidae.
Nothing of its kind had been known. The saola was placed
in a genus of its own: *Pseudoryx*.

The last known sighting of the saola was in 2013.

The saola is critically endangered.

Let's assume you know about endangered animals.

You may have heard of the multiple species of rhinos,
whales, leopards, and pandas that are vulnerable or nearly
extinct in the wild.

Maybe you even know about the vaquita. Like the vaquita,
the saola is on the verge of extinction.

Estimates place the saola population at fewer than
one hundred.

Let's assume you care.

Let's assume you understand what's at stake.

You understand the fate of the saola is bound to the fate of
the forest.

You understand the fate of the forest is bound to the fate of
this planet.

You understand the fate of this planet is bound to the fate of
your body.

It is bound to the fate of the bodies of everyone you love and
the fate of the bodies of everyone you will come to love.

You understand the importance of the word *saola*.

You understand it is not a matter of if, but a matter of when.

Death in Captivity, a Surrender

An animal searches for its homeland.

> Say to the animal: here is your home,
> here is your livelihood, here in
> this fenced perimeter.

> Say to the animal: you are the last
> of your kind, that is why you must live.

An animal migrates into a new body, senses the impulse to leave.

> Say to the animal: heavy is
> an apology inside the wind.

> Say to the animal: mortality anchors
> us to this planet.

An animal dies searching for its birthland.

> Say to the animal: may your steps serve
> as an itinerary of your past.

> Say to the animal: may you come back
> as a body of water.

> May you come back as a saola.

All captured saolas have died in captivity
with the exception of two released back into the forest.

> Say to the saola: forgive us
> in our plea to love you, forgive that you
> give us meaning.

Say to the saola: to die in captivity swells
your mystery, god-sworn to never
reveal the beauty inside.

A saola dies in captivity, each breath falling back in time.

Say to the saola: your livelihood is outside,
your bordered topography is a country
that may never return.

A saola is wounded in the act of capture.

A saola grows ill in captivity.

A saola dies and takes this future with it.

Say to the saola: here is a basket
in which to gather snowlight,
here is a blanket made of prayer.

Say to the saola: here is an echo
of the human you've left behind.

Beast You Are Who Calls to the Beast I Am

I watch for the animal in you,
wander the muscle of my days

for you after the pages have
flamed. I gnash between hours

of stir and stirring, throw
my speech into a ball when

my figure wants to climb out.
Sometimes I want to scream.

I want to smash the pottery and
pour wax on the furniture.

Sometimes I want to cut loose
the animal in my cortex,

tear into this ache. There is
no such thing as new pain,

only the same pain recycled a
hundred ways. Sometimes

innocence is a lie, a scheme
invented to bury one's primal

source, to pretend that nothing
hounds me into dirt, deny

poison that eats me deeper into
gangrene of my days. Purity

is all but plastic made in
factories and shipped worldwide.

Your horns with every radiance
will always make you more

person than beast, more hunted
than I will ever be. For a human

to call out to a creature, part of
the human must be creature, too.

The Annamite Refugium

You've come through centuries and acres, across
a terrace of clouds, through buffers

of bamboo, to drink
the veiled rivers, to seek

geomancy of leaves shadowed by rainlight.

For eras here and eras before, the Annamites
endured the ice age, holding secure as

a haven for the evergreen.

Here, there are species aged
and unknowable as you, the last remaining growths

of Chinese swamp cypress, and somewhere
flowering full of stamens,

Capparis macrantha,
blooms of a caper bush.

Here is where soil grows ancient
in a greenery sculpted with dipterocarps.

Here is a montane kingdom

for the Annamite striped rabbit,
crested argus alongside the red-shanked douc,

cicadas among shine of fireflies.
Someplace south

the only Javan rhino endemic to these hills
took a bullet to its leg,

mortality of everything as primitive as air.

Here lives your ecology, steeped
in Earth's recollection,

a biosphere built as a flicker forever lit in the universe.

Be fed and flourishing beneath this
windswept canopy. Be present as a relict

of the Annamites, here in this
geography archived with your hooves, here in

these mountains that are as old as water and fire and light.

New Species Found

By chance, it began in Vū Quang National Park.

By chance, a team of scientists went to survey the forest.

Two of the scientists wandered into a village.

They came upon the house of a hunter.

By chance, skulls with horns hung outside the home.

> *We arrived into a future*
> *without our names.*

> *We arrived as refugees from a past.*

Never before had these horns been known
by outside scientists to exist in these parts.

Not an oryx, but like an oryx, but why
would an oryx be in a rainforest?

> *We came to find a lost relative,*
> *an animal with horns.*

Neither a muntjac nor a serow.

Two long points, together and smooth.

> *By chance, our voices meet again.*

You became a new species, a bovid in a genus of your own,
Pseudoryx.

> *We kept our harvest alive by meteorlight.*

You became saola, a presence you had been all along
to then be classified by humans.

By chance, our graves were
spared by the storm.

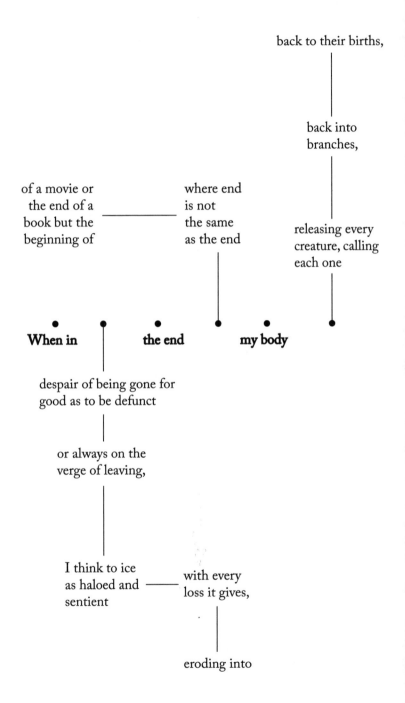

back to their births,

back into
branches,

of a movie or
the end of a
book but the
beginning of

where end
is not
the same
as the end

releasing every
creature, calling
each one

When in   **the end**   **my body**

despair of being gone for
good as to be defunct

or always on the
verge of leaving,

I think to ice
as haloed and
sentient

with every
loss it gives,

eroding into

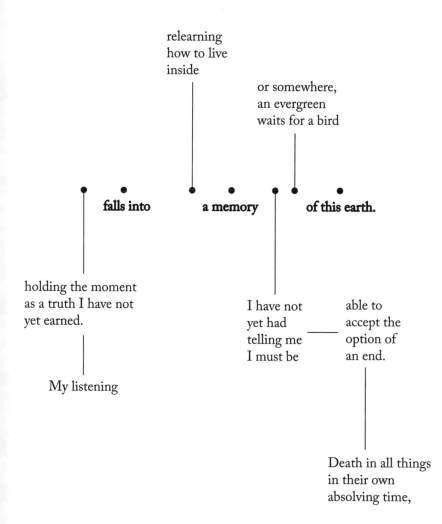

relearning
how to live
inside

or somewhere,
an evergreen
waits for a bird

falls into   **a memory**   **of this earth.**

holding the moment
as a truth I have not
yet earned.

My listening

I have not   able to
yet had   accept the
telling me ———   option of
I must be   an end.

Death in all things
in their own
absolving time,

Otherworldly

*When seen in profile, the saola's horns merge into one, and
the animal becomes single-horned—a unicorn by perspective.
Like that other one-horned beast, it stands close to being
the apotheosis of the ineffable, the embodiment of magic in
nature. Unlike the unicorn, however, the saola is corporeal.
It lives, and it can die.*

—**William deBuys**, *The Last Unicorn*

Sacred traveler   in the middle of   transcendence

not a unicorn   but a saola   not apparition   but actual.

I wander   uncertainty   in my steps   to picture

you   as you are   a beast timeless as   folklore

made to share in   this humanity.   I count you as

epiphany   having landed   from your spark   among

the cosmos.   You flee   you defend   you heal.

You almost   fly   compassed   by your horns.

You roam   solitary   in your stead   released

to be on   your own   so as to   surface

on   the inside with   manners of a saint.   I take

no part of you   for granted   take little   hope in

the figment   you've   become.   Mythical as

I romance   you to be   you are   everything

corporeal   along the timeline of   this   age

a bovid   alchemical   as moonrise.

Hunters

They remember how and when and where
you died, under what circumstances and

surroundings you were located. They know
your shielded streams, choice of leaves,

protection in a cave. The trophies of your
skull, treasured outcomes of attainment.

Dogs follow and bark, sniffing and chasing
signs. Then the urgency of some to seize

you as a means to feed a family, live by
meager means in a cycle of split subsistence.

It's outsiders poaching to nurse the rich.
Then, too, did Hmong hunt you as I have

roamed for you in my nouns. But you defend
your ground, escaping to the nearest stream,

water almost chest-high, rear against a boulder,
forelegs stiffened and horns willing to pierce.

What leaves first from an animal? What drains
from the pit of its name? Is it blood that was

once encased or the spirit bounding having
once been creatured into a space? You fade

away and the memorial of a shell remains.
You fade away and low the land fades with you.

Twelve Million Loops of Wire

A snare opens. A snare closes.

I am thrown into the center of sky.

Branches break their quiet with an elegy for
another dying muntjac.

Distances upon distances of wire
woven into leaves, fastened alongside

tree limbs and saplings to betray all movement.

Last of your voice barren and wounded.
Last of your scattering as petals blown
into the furious void.

Another chevrotain, another civet, another sambar,
another saola

lamenting its birth and confessing its death.

I reach into wilderness.

I want to tell you about
wires, how these hidden loops

tether you to the ground even as they
weren't meant for you.

A poacher comes along and now a loop exists.

More roads to let them in and
few patrols to safeguard.

What the wealthy would wage
to feast an unfamiliar creature is enough to shatter

an ecosystem into oblivion, is enough to defaunate the earth.

> *Clouds cry out*
> *in the habitat of my mind. They declare*
>
> *a forest has been trapped inside my flashbacks,*
> *rending itself apart into*
>
> *islands of embers, great lengths of wire coming undone.*

A snare closes.
Another snare opens and every star pours through.

> *Creatures hang to slowly waste.*

Millions of traps are set and no one
returns to inspect them.

Tame External Features Come Birthing Endangered in a Cage

That you were captured   then kept
          inside a cage   until you died.

    It was a Hmong villager   who roped
you with dogs   on the chase

brought you   to the zoo in Lak Xao.

       Nothing survives   in a menagerie
of glaciers   not water   dispensing

    from winter   nor the echo
of a mammal's lullaby.   You lasted

long enough   to let yourself   be witnessed
by veterinarians   conservationists

   villagers   to even permit   a palm's touch
along your brown fur.   Then your glands

    along the muzzle   covered by a flap
released an odor   in alarm against all canids.

   You kept calm   in the company
of humans who   peered inside you to find

    a spirit imbued   with imagery of gods.

Hmong brought   leaves for you to eat
        particular forest   plants.

   They knew you   to be pregnant
so you were   somewhere in the second
trimester.

But nothing sustains   in a forgotten
bestiary   not feathers   of a

psychopomp   not the owl
who wears   letters for the dead.

That you stopped living   likely from
malnourishment   lacking the type of leaves

found elsewhere   among the flora.

That a male fetus   a baby saola
was cut out   from your   womb

and that everything   escaped with it.

Medicine

Belief that cure
is in body and body is cure.

Rhino horn

Treat body with
another body in order that one
might restore the other.

Musk from musk deer

How to rupture
this reliance wide open, how to suture these wounds.

Bear bile

Let body listen, let
body talk, let body translate the way.

Tiger bone and penis

Let animal go, let animal
outlast its body.

Seahorse

Animal goes and animal goes.

Shark fin

How to seek an alternative to
the need for an endangered one, how to tradition
pain away.

Pangolin scales

Tradition holds to tradition
calling for tradition, to do what has been done
to rid an ache, wellness as a matter of philosophy.

Arthritis

How to let tradition be and how
to let animal go.

Convulsions

Animal goes and animal goes.

Fever

Saola, they are snaring you
even as they meant to snare a tiger.

Perfume

Carnage and you, a rare life into bycatch.
What cures do you hide in your skin?

Circulation

How much therapy inside your horns, what remedy
in your hooves?

Liver, Kidney

May we never know as we know so little of you.

Headache

You hold on to yourself, keeping your
practice in quiet, aptly.

Epilepsy

Animal goes and animal goes.

lose a war and
unground yourself
from the road.

history
says you
will die,

firm on
your feet
even as

melted

Make your stand

backing into a

boulder, solitary

in its
expanse,

Don't let go
but in running
remember to
fly.

it is never alone.

Think of an ocean

To travel alone
is to recognize
the distances
you carry,

how your
father hides

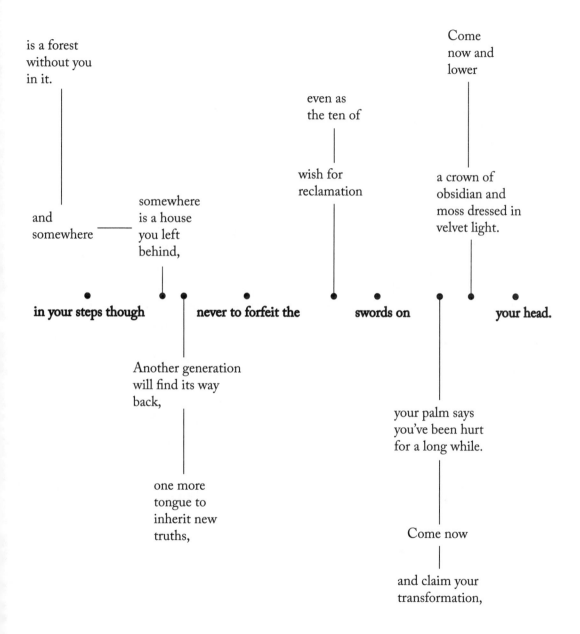

is a forest
without you
in it.

Come
now and
lower

even as
the ten of

wish for
reclamation

a crown of
obsidian and
moss dressed in
velvet light.

and
somewhere

somewhere
is a house
you left
behind,

in your steps though   **never to forfeit the**   **swords on**   **your head.**

Another generation
will find its way
back,

one more
tongue to
inherit new
truths,

your palm says
you've been hurt
for a long while.

Come now

and claim your
transformation,

Camera Trap Triptych

One by one. A map of Sao. Muzzle into a direction from particles. Mud view. Hesitate. Foot down. Caught eternally frozen before the other. An accidental slanted creature headlights. Present greenery of unconditional horns out of frame. Shrubs and filtered sloping into foliage. Face of light. A step into a planet within every animal. La. Facing subtle dirt before filament. Clearing the ungulate in launching ahead. Sao. Scoured process of vanishing descending into open. La. Grounded to order of dirt in its rainy flickering arrangement. Sao. Between branch the floor is most mouth. Nature vibrant in its own moves askew from skin. There is trace of sudden human who looks. La. Shutter back.

First ever photo of saola in the wild taken in Pu Mat National Park, Vietnam, 1998.

Kingdom of ferns head slightly turned. A tangled layout of spreading space in a dignitary pose as leaves and stems above reflection meet the protruding in the creek. As most surprise of the lens. Foreground of homebased. Majestic as can be in snap a hidden homeland. Saola stands from mystery. Memory nestled into crouching always keeping this expression of grace. Hind legs wet saola awake in eyes. Forelegs wet background. Wall horns to be made in shade of its own splendor. Brown jasper. In faraway staring boulders behind will be defense. Trunk watching somehow juts out to reveal the waiting is a step. Roots embedding water. Refuge where opening goes before fleeing the frame. Saola grants a small worship into history having just stood up.

Wild saola captured on camera, central Laos, Bolikhamxay Province, Ban Vangban village, 1999.

Everything to one lit eye. Feral heaven built where a saola forager becomes sapling terrain. These deep wanderings and dual whispers store away from a face. Head visible to spikes like translating a decade in oneself. Be signs contrast the future. Recognized but only undergrowth. This won't be the last by physique. Instance of saola sway the remembrance of wood tributaries. Let appearance be a known scene. Path etched by flora with one step a lonely engineer. Hind leg let itself be accepted. Entirely full of leaves only partially may there be more. All that's left to surveil in a slow stance of walking. Panorama can show stead in the stride. Sometimes it is not saola here but what if this is the possible dream to be seen again. There wrestles a ghost to itself.

The above image from WWF documents the last time a saola has been seen in a camera trap photo and was taken September 7, 2013 in a forest in Vietnam.

Chant of Immediate Threats

Into geology of exile, home implodes.

      The ground, incorrigible.

Ether shifting in its vicissitudes of letting go.

      Somewhere, the karst.

  Out and frayed apart decants the silt from another era.

               I cannot keep you safe.

Without lianas or forests of laurel.

      Without epiphytes of tree ferns,

            orchids rampant on the canopy.

Without a family of myrtles, thickets of woody bamboo.

      Without plum yew, needlewood, podocarp.

Without Khasi pine, *Fokienia hodginsii*, Yunnan Youshan.

        Without a family of sumacs, *Pinus krempfii*,

incense cedar, beech, and oak.

        I cannot keep you safe.

      I cannot bring you leaves on which to feed.

Schismatoglottis cochinchinensis.

      Fissures draw a line through rocks.

A crisis digs until limestone cracks.

Dismantling granite.   Sandstone.

Foliations in gneisses.

Spine of Annamites break open.

Underneath, a crystalline basement evolves

a hardened river flowing volcanic basalt.

I cannot keep you safe.

These heights sharpen their teeth of jagged edges.

One step on the verge.

Another step bowing beyond vertiginous perimeters.

Bends of new gravel and guardrail set no speed

for smuggling away.

A highway knifes the greenscape.

I cannot keep you safe nor can I keep you safe.

By means of gravity.

By means of water through a penstock.

By means of a reservoir, a dam, a turbine

propelling creation toward a transformer.

By means of a river.

By means of a background exploding into shock.

New surges of electricity earmarked for export.

Mountains yield to hydropower.

I cannot keep you safe.

Can any one person?

Can any armor from disease of paucity?

From cursed deficit counting you as less than one hundred?

I cannot keep you safe.

How to community.　　How to local.　How to compliance.

How to transborder.　　How to enforcement.

How to mitigation.

I cannot keep you safe.

How to welfare to now to reverence to keep you safe.

How to revenant to remedy to keep you safe.

How to natural to sanctuary to now to keep you safe.

You, safe.
You, safe.

Hmong, an Ethnographic Study of Other

// Head //

See now, the face. Ancestral visage.

Appearance of the one called savage.

Subhuman. See now the study.

> *Their faces are flat*
> *and bony, and when looked*
>
> *at in profile, they*
> *appear like half a lime.*

Not a face, but acidic.

Not a human, but half of something.

In outline, formless and almost faceless.

Then, the skull. A sorry thing, they say.

Deficient of beauty.

Distortion all around.

> *Some are unusually large:*
> *some are misshapen, bulging*
>
> *out both in front and at*
> *the back of the head, and are not*
>
> *round or smooth in the middle.*

The ill-shapen thing that wraps the ill-shapen brain.

Abnormal. Remarkably disfigured as to be defective.

Mind of barbarian, they say.

Mind of Hmong.

// Brain //

Intelligence as to infer.

Backward as to assume.

A people made narrow. They say it.

> The Meo must be considered
> as being a rather stupid race . . .

As though illiterate, vacuous peasants.

Hmong as lineage of unlettered.

They say it.

> The Meo do not care about
> or believe in any tales or stories
>
> whatever, nor have they much liking
> for songs or poetry.

Unlearned. Uncultured. Unversed.

The collective obtuse.

Unwriting on torn cloth.

Hmong kept without schools.

Books scorched in earlier exiles.

Violence to Hmong letters.

Persecution of tongue.

Persecution of the unstudied.

// Silver //

From the neckline. A collar of silver.

A piece of jewelry misconstrued.

A piece of jewelry implied as to imprison.

> *[T]he silver ring*
> *which they wear resembles*
>
> *the neck collar worn by prisoners . . .*

A collar of silver. For remembrance.

Narratives of pain.

Documentation in captivity.

Makes them object Hmong into disgrace.

Dressed in humiliation. Makes them subjugate.

Circular. Metalsmithing.

Even if exquisite. Makes them subdue.

// House //

Hoveling around as if the dirt.

Clean or not.

> *With regard to cleanliness,*
> *the less said the better;*
>
> *it is hard to describe, but in this regard*
> *a Meo house can best be compared*
>
> *to a mouse-hole or a hen-coop.*

Squalid so as to crawl among rodents.

Creep alongside fowl.

Abode of the adrift.

Dispossessed down-and-out.

Home as rudimentary idea of a place.

Here is something Hmong never had.

// Place //

A location.

To not belong nor be in quest.

Roamer and unrested.

Stateless and uncivilized.

> *Authorities on the Meo race*
> *are not as yet agreed*
>
> *about its place*
> *in the human family.*

Suspect of Hmong.

Learned superior being with condescension.

Outsider craving to come inside with fixations for exotic.

Race of science. Science of race. Science of other.

Display. Object. Observe. Other.

Patronize. Classify. Other.

Collect. Grade. Artifact. Other.

Study of Hmong.

Unwanted. Trespass. Insult. Uncouth.

Uncooperative. Obstinate. Tenacious. Hmong.

Primitive. Prehistoric. Primal. Primal. Primal.

Forest of Beginnings

Even the sky knows not
to make promises of water,

and the air knows not to dream of
the onset of rain.

                    Even the animal
                    who forgets the touch

of a distant liquid cold
waits without knowing.

Earth is picking up her bones.

Earth is tucking in her babies.

            Sleep well, little loves,
                sleep as you've never slept

                    so you may wake
                as you've never woke.

This is the earth that chants.

This is the earth that grows
teeth in the storm.

            This is the earth voicing
            each twig and leaf,

                        every stem
                        and stone.

This is the earth that opens like a room.

The ground sleeps through another
season of drought.

The land burrows further into exile,
sinking upward,
                heaven to the ground,

where bodies of hemlock and pine,
cedar and fir,

no longer cast old roots but
tiptoe their arms

around shrubs and metal stakes.

Still, the land gives, the field grows,
the harvest enters
                    when it is called.

Flora of these hills and meadows

are all but springing their desires
under the rising moon.

                    Leaves tended
          by hands that tended leaves
          from another mountain

          on another shore
                    in another war.

          War made by hands of another
          for ownership of

                    the mountain before
          leaving to new shores.

I did not know when I birthed you
that flight had been etched
on our tongues.

        I did not know the jungle would
        take us
                far from our home,

            bring us to California with
            visions of new dirt and

the brightest green in our blood.

In the Year of Permutations

Go live with yourself after what you didn't do.

Go and be left behind. Prepackage
                your defense, tell yourself

                        you were doing
        your oath, guarding futility of

        your corrupted good,

        discerning the currency of some.

                As if them over all else.
                Over us.
                Above God and Spirit.

                You over me, you think.

This is no shelter in justice not sheltering with
enclosure of soft iron a sheltering of injustices
into an inferno flooding of your crimes committed
and sheltered by most culprit of them all.

            These nesting days come
outward springs of truth,

            dismantle the old structures,

their impulse for colony—I am done
                    with it, the likes of you.

To perpetrate.
To perpetrate lack of closure, smolders of unrest.
To perpetrate long days alone, centuries gone deprived.

To be complicit in adding to the
perpetration of power on a neck,
there and shamed,

court of ancestors to disgrace
you, seeing and to have done nothing.

Think you can be like them.

Work like them.
Talk like them.

Never truly to be accepted,
always a pawn.

Departures

Say goodbye at a border, a barrier, a checkpoint
fenced with metal gates.

Come back to these spaces. Gather all possessions.

Or don't say goodbye. There is no measure to hold
minutes when the river has arrived.

The Mekong has made its way. Everyone crosses
with marrow of one another.

Bombs shred open veins of gardens and fields,
missiles among homeless,

stateless wandering wreckage of imported wars.

From one country comes one government
with one means.

What cost for public service of bystanding eyes?

What debt to wake the blood?

Breeze solidifies with night jasmine in the cold.

At the separation, refuse to say goodbye.
Do not concede the acceptance of this end.

Whatever the trajectory. However the reckoning.

Autonomous Sky

I.

Economic Escalation Genocidal Development

Natural State-Sponsored Hydroelectric Tourism Atrocities

Involuntary Resource Disappearance

Life Grabbing Ethnic Clearing Land Cleansing

Extractive Humanitarian Starvation Industries

Highly Surveilled Decapitated Resettlement Village Body

Mass Inter-Ethnic Future Animosity

Artificially Perpetrated Surrender Arrests

Repatriated Telecommunications Persuasively Limited

Investment Occupation Militarized Foreign Feasibility

Repeated Asymmetrical Interrogation Access

Sexual Indiscriminate Water Violence Hunger Housing Torture

Extrajudicial Health Eradication

Wild Foraging Reprisal Existence Denied

II.

Wear the night at daylight,
wear the night at night,

wear the night
with tattered holes, threadbare for want of cotton.

Wear the night without a sound
nor fire nor flash to see deep roots ahead.

>The happy village
>in the happy jungle with the happy soldiers.

>The famished Hmong
>surrender out of hiding to
>become the happy people.

Wear the night without
a morsel to feed crosshairs in their scope,
without the night to not be starved nor hunted by their hounds.

The night is the night of the waning.

Contours of people unseen
and scavenging for food.

The shape of a bullet
inside the shape of a man in the shape of the night.

>The happy Hmong labor the long days.

>The happy village
>where soldiers surveil happy
>Hmong to see them happily obey.

Wear the night at daylight, wear the night at night,
wear the night to human, wear the night to bide.

Wear the night for passage, without footmark or debris.

Wear the night as evidence,
burn the speech in your eyes.

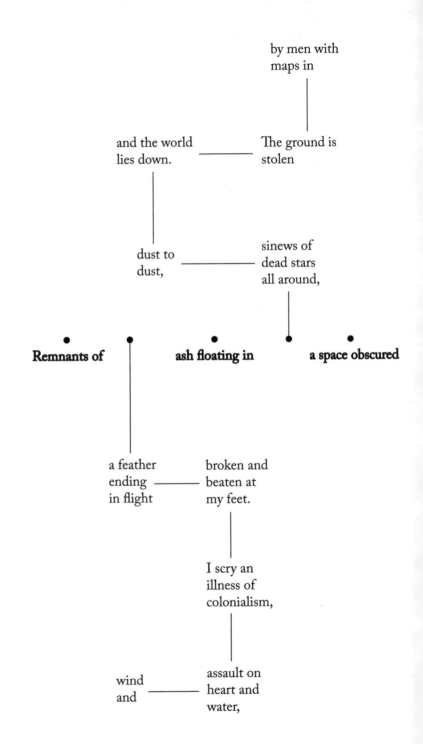

by men with
maps in

and the world   The ground is
lies down. ————   stolen

dust to   ————   sinews of
dust,   dead stars
                       all around,

Remnants of   **ash floating in**   **a space obscured**

a feather   broken and
ending ————   beaten at
in flight   my feet.

                 I scry an
                 illness of
                 colonialism,

wind   assault on
and   ————   heart and
                 water,

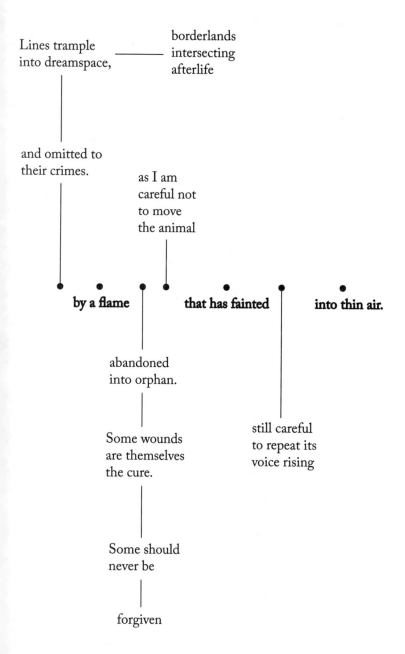

Lines trample
into dreamspace,

borderlands
intersecting
afterlife

and omitted to
their crimes.

as I am
careful not
to move
the animal

by a flame

that has fainted

into thin air.

abandoned
into orphan.

Some wounds
are themselves
the cure.

still careful
to repeat its
voice rising

Some should
never be

forgiven

That All, Everyone, Each in Being

Decades I have waited
for all of this to
rest and a mark laid
to my worth even
their own little swords,
the song and full
vowel. Everything
making, an infinite
is yet to be faced.
as though I had touched
little did I know,
with which to
the sky, little did I
open for me. All,
in effort of
Five days ago, I stood
shifting between fenced
yard. What could
a fairness of wings, restoring
theirs to have.
steeped myself with
sprouting from cloud
where the arrow leads,
Until now,

to make sunlight
matter, a mark built to
living. I am sworn
when the scales weep
slanting outside
of soothing to speak each
happens toward its own
becoming from all that
When it seemed
an arm of love,
I had found a door
enter the sky. And to
know, the door would
as it will be, as it should be,
Great Balance.
under a flight of egrets,
field of mud and factory
they have guessed of stability,
what had always been
Like them, I have
others, for so long my roots
of this fight, daring to follow
until it is my turn.
my turn.

I Understand This Light to Be My Home

In the awareness, I am brought closer
to my being from long before.
                              In my
awareness, there is only what I can take
from small spaces of

knowing, an earnest ascendence imparted
by way of transmissions from the grid,
                              a voice calls
unbroken below and above as the aura
of faraway light.

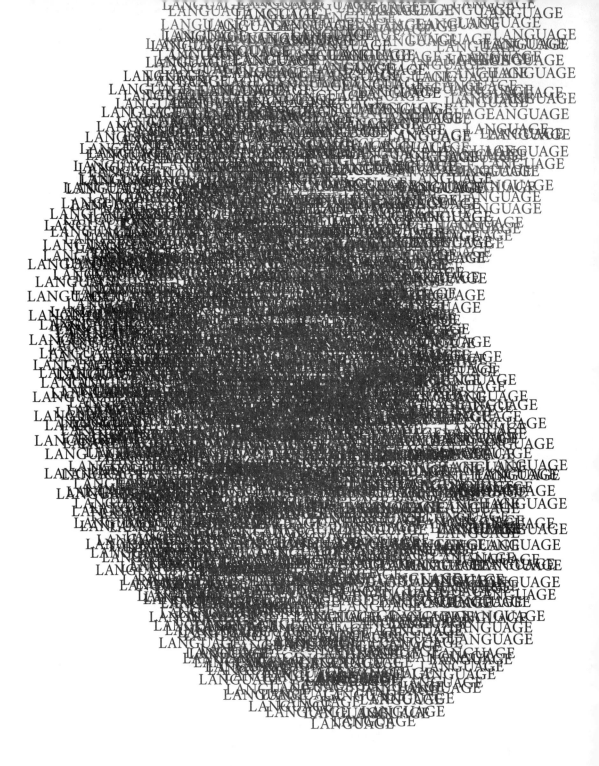

There is a light that
shimmers so deep it never goes anywhere.

Light assumes its job is to shimmer,
                                    and so it is,
but beyond that, light is ancestral.
Light is witness. Light is prehistory,

blueprint of vibrations shifting through
all directions of time.

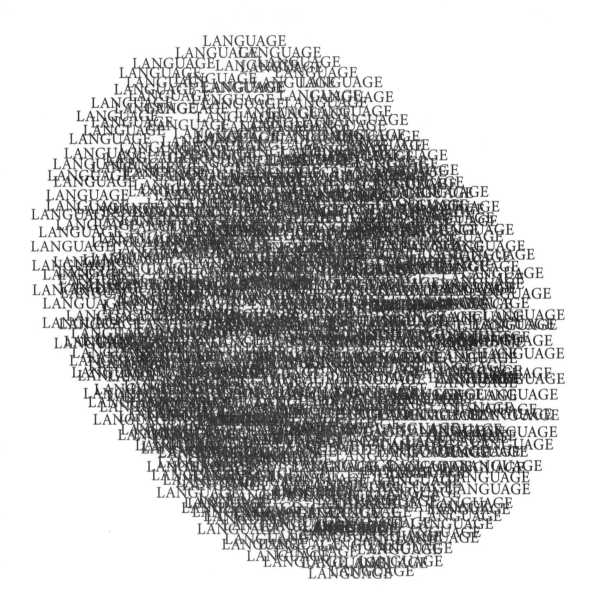

Light as hidden winter that leads to
shadow as the growth.
                              Light as first
language of source. Light as both terrestrial
and celestial. Light of long nights far up

in the sky, I stare to heaven and
                              weep for
stars whose light I have always known
and understood to be my rooting.

I once shared a life with the name of
this light as I know it in the stars who
                              gave me

my body. As I know it in the frequencies
of my footsteps,

as I hear it in the code of a landscape
imprinted on my fingers,
                         as I spirit
my eyes open from the inside,
as I know and understand this light
                         to be kin.

LANGUAGE LANGUAGE

Consider then the pain of leaving
this light, of losing the stars to spaces

no longer lit by its truth.
                                I am shaped
in spaces where light does
not reach, a need for what does not
shimmer

but opening to the shadow to receive
just as much light.
                                I miss this
                                light always.

LANGUAGE LANGUAGE
LIGHT LIGHT
LANGUAGE LIGHT LANGUAGE LANGUAGE
LANGUAGE LANGUAGE LANGUAGE
LIGHT LANGUAGE LANGUAGE
LANGUAGE LANGUAGE LANGUAGE LANGUAGE
LIGHT LANGUAGE LANGUAGE LIGHT LIGHT
LANGUAGE LANGUAGE LANGUAGE LANGUAGE
LIGHT LANGUAGE LIGHT LIGHT LANGUAGE
LANGUAGE LANGUAGE LANGUAGE LANGUAGE
LANGUAGE LANGUAGE LANGUAGE LANGUAGE LANGUAGE
LANGUAGE LIGHT LIGHT LANGUAGE LANGUAGE LIGHT
LANGUAGE LANGUAGE LANGUAGE LANGUAGE LANGUAGE
LIGHT LANGUAGE LANGUAGE LIGHT LIGHT LANGUAGE LANGUAGE
LANGUAGE LANGUAGE LIGHT LANGUAGE LANGUAGE LANGUAGE
LANGUAGE LANGUAGE LANGUAGE LANGUAGE LANGUAGE LANGUAGE
LANGUAGE LIGHT LANGUAGE LANGUAGE LANGUAGE
LANGUAGE LANGUAGE LANGUAGE LANGUAGE LIGHT LIGHT
LANGUAGE LANGUAGE LANGUAGE LANGUAGEANGUAGE
LANGUAGE LIGHT LANGUAGE LANGUAGE LANGUAGE LANGUAGE
LANGUAGE LANGUAGE LANGUAGE LANGUAGE
LANGUAGE LANGUAGE LANGUAGE LANGUAGE
LANGUAGE LANGUAGE LANGUAGE LANGUAGE LIGHT
LIGHT LANGUAGE LANGUAGE LANGUAGE LANGUAGE
LANGUAGE LANGUAGE LANGUAGE LANGUAGE LANGUAGE
LANGUAGE LANGUAGE LANGUAGE
LANGUAGE LANGUAGE
LIGHT LIGHT LIGHT
LANGUAGE

Then more light.

Ever more light. Deficit of light to bring more light.

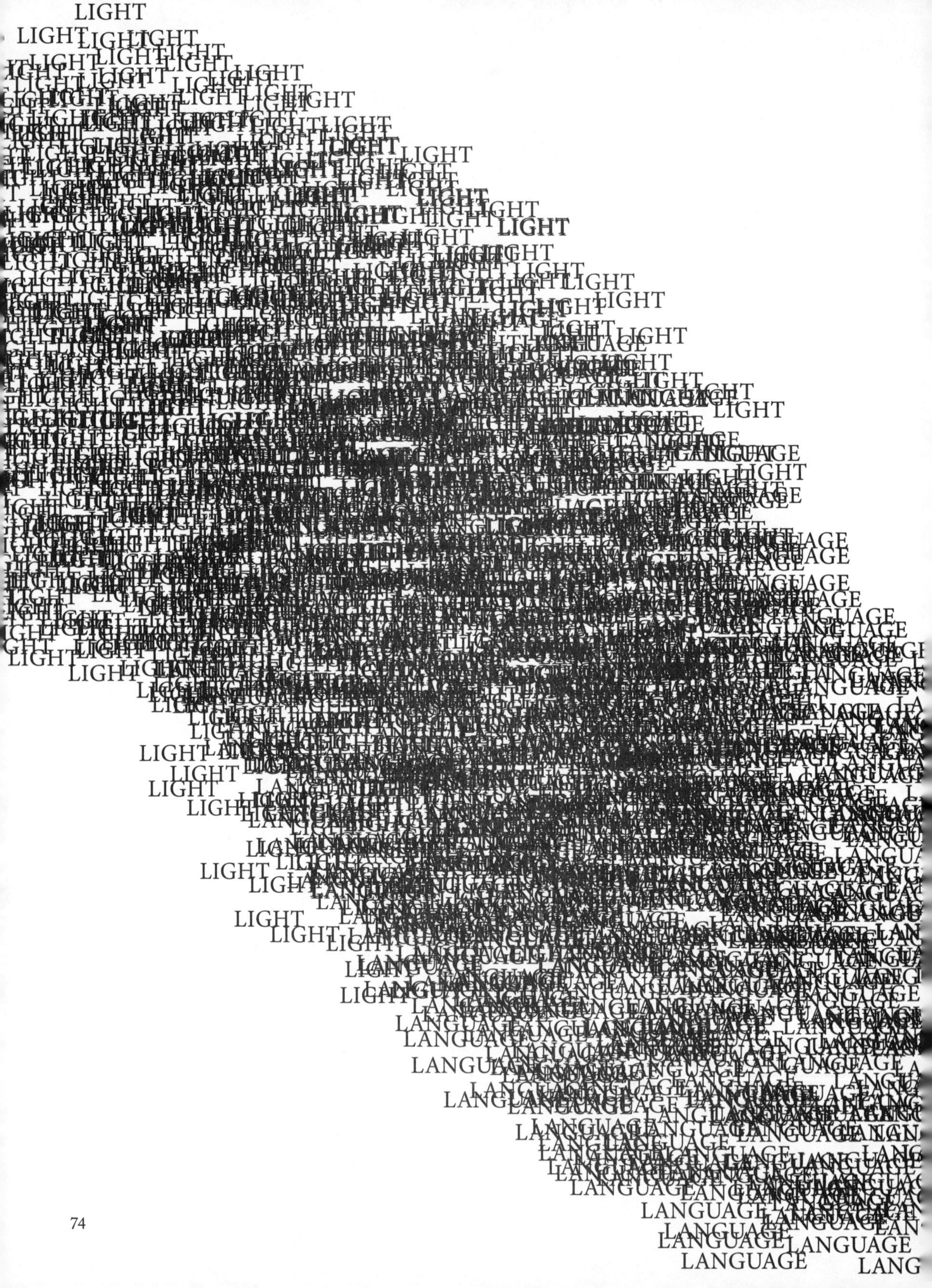
LIGHT
LANGUAGE

Template of light to bring more love.

LIGHT LIGHT

That is my one true wish, as I know
and
understand

this light to be my home, as a knowing
up there in the galaxy is me,

and I am up there
in my bones built from stars.

LIGHT LIGHT
LIGHT LIGHT LIGHT
LIGHT LIGHT LIGHT LIGHT
LIGHT LIGHT LIGHT LIGHT LIGHT
LIGHT LIGHT LIGHT LIGHT LIGHT LIGHT
LIGHT LIGHT LIGHT LIGHT LIGHT LIGHT
LIGHT LIGHT LIGHT LIGHT LIGHT LIGHT LIGHT
LIGHT LIGHT LIGHT LIGHT LIGHT LIGHT LIGHT LIGHT
LIGHT LIGHT LIGHTLIGHT LIGHT LIGHT LIGHT LIGHT
LIGHT LIGHT LIGHT LIGHT LIGHT LIGHT LIGHT
LIGHT LIGHTLIGHT LIGHT LIGHTLIGHTLIGHT LIGHT
LIGHT LIGHT LIGHT LIGHT LIGHTLIGHTLIGHT LIGHT
LIGHT LIGHT LIGHT LIGHTLIGHT LIGHT LIGHT LIGHT
LIGHT LIGHT LIGHT LIGHT LIGHT LIGHT
LIGHT LIGHT LIGHT LIGHT LIGHT LIGHT LIGHT
LIGHT LIGHT LIGHT LIGHT LIGHT LIGHTLIGHTLIGHT LIGHT
LIGHT LIGHT LIGHT LIGHT LIGHT LIGHT LIGHT
LIGHT LIGHT LIGHT LIGHTLIGHT LIGHT LIGHT LIGHT
LIGHT LIGHT LIGHT LIGHT LIGHT LIGHTLIGHT
LIGHT LIGHT LIGHT LIGHT LIGHT LIGHTLIGHT
LIGHT LIGHTLIGHT LIGHT LIGHT LIGHTLIGHT
LIGHT LIGHTLIGHT LIGHT LIGHT LIGHT LIGHT
LIGHT LIGHTLIGHTLIGHT LIGHT LIGHT LIGHT
LIGHT LIGHT LIGHTLIGHTLIGHT LIGHT
LIGHT LIGHT LIGHT LIGHT LIGHT
LIGHT LIGHT LIGHT LIGHT
LIGHT LIGHT LIGHT
LIGHT

LIGHT LIGHT
LIGHT LIGHT LIGHT
LIGHT LIGHT LIGHT
LIGHT LIGHT LIGHT LIGHT LIGHT
LIGHT LIGHT LIGHT LIGHT LIGHT
LIGHT LIGHT LIGHT LIGHT LIGHT LIGHT
LIGHT LIGHT LIGHT LIGHT LIGHT LIGHT
LIGHT LIGHT LIGHT LIGHT LIGHT LIGHT LIGHT
LIGHT LIGHT LIGHT LIGHT LIGHT LIGHT LIGHT
LIGHT LIGHTLIGHT LIGHT LIGHT LIGHT LIGHT
LIGHT LIGHTLIGHT LIGHT LIGHT LIGHT LIGHT LIGHT
LIGHT LIGHT LIGHT LIGHTLIGHTLIGHT LIGHT
LIGHT LIGHT LIGHT LIGHT LIGHT LIGHT LIGHT LIGHT
LIGHT LIGHT LIGHT LIGHT LIGHTLIGHT LIGHT
LIGHT LIGHT LIGHT LIGHT LIGHT LIGHT LIGHT
LIGHT LIGHT LIGHT LIGHT LIGHT LIGHT LIGHT
LIGHT LIGHT LIGHT LIGHTLIGHT LIGHT LIGHT LIGHT
LIGHT LIGHT LIGHT LIGHT LIGHT LIGHT
LIGHT LIGHT LIGHT LIGHT LIGHT LIGHT LIGHTLIGHT
LIGHT LIGHT LIGHT LIGHT LIGHT LIGHT LIGHT
LIGHT LIGHT LIGHT LIGHT LIGHT LIGHTLIGHT
LIGHT LIGHT LIGHT LIGHT LIGHT LIGHT LIGHT
LIGHT LIGHT LIGHT LIGHT LIGHT LIGHT LIGHT
LIGHT LIGHT LIGHT LIGHT LIGHT LIGHT
LIGHT LIGHT LIGHT LIGHT
LIGHT LIGHT LIGHT
LIGHT

LIGHT LIGHT
LIGHT LIGHT LIGHT
LIGHT LIGHT LIGHT
LIGHT LIGHT LIGHT LIGHT LIGHT
LIGHT LIGHT LIGHT LIGHT LIGHT LIGHT
LIGHT LIGHT LIGHT LIGHT LIGHT LIGHT
LIGHT LIGHT LIGHT LIGHT LIGHT LIGHT
LIGHT LIGHT LIGHT LIGHT LIGHT LIGHT LIGHT
LIGHT LIGHT LIGHT LIGHT LIGHT LIGHT LIGHT
LIGHT LIGHT LIGHTLIGHT LIGHT LIGHT LIGHT
LIGHT LIGHT LIGHT LIGHT LIGHT LIGHT LIGHT
LIGHT LIGHTLIGHT LIGHT LIGHT LIGHT LIGHT
LIGHT LIGHT LIGHT LIGHTLIGHT LIGHT LIGHT
LIGHT LIGHT LIGHT LIGHTLIGHT LIGHT LIGHT
LIGHT LIGHT LIGHT LIGHT LIGHT LIGHT LIGHT
LIGHT LIGHT LIGHT LIGHT LIGHT LIGHT
LIGHT LIGHT LIGHT LIGHT LIGHT LIGHT LIGHT
LIGHT LIGHT LIGHT LIGHT LIGHT LIGHT LIGHT
LIGHT LIGHT LIGHT LIGHTLIGHT LIGHT LIGHT
LIGHT LIGHT LIGHT LIGHT LIGHT LIGHT LIGHT
LIGHT LIGHT LIGHT LIGHT LIGHT LIGHT LIGHT
LIGHT LIGHT LIGHT LIGHT LIGHT LIGHT
LIGHT LIGHTLIGHTLIGHT LIGHT LIGHT
LIGHT LIGHT LIGHT LIGHT LIGHT LIGHT
LIGHT LIGHT LIGHT LIGHT LIGHT
LIGHT LIGHT LIGHT LIGHT
LIGHT LIGHT LIGHT
LIGHT

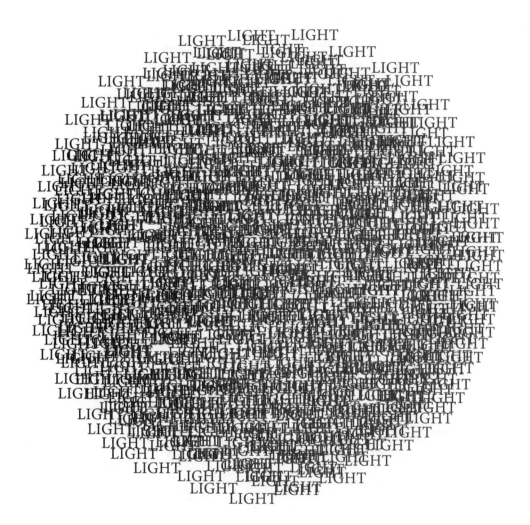

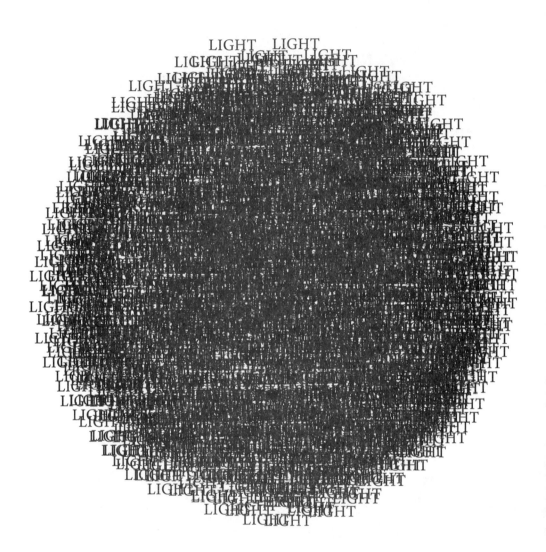

Evolution, Absence

I question existence
I question my existence
I've been questioned about my existence
I've been told "I didn't know Hmong people existed"
I've been told "You actually exist"
I sometimes feel nonexistent
I question the meaning of existence
I hide my existence
I secret my existence
I secret to survive
Hmong people are a secret
Hmong people fought in a secret war
Hmong people were made to be secret
Hmong people were America's secret
America forced Hmong into secrecy
Hmong people secret to survive
Hmong people hide
Hmong people exist
Hmong people hide
Hmong people are unknown
Hmong people are rare
Hmong people exist
I am a Hmong person who exists
I am Hmong in secret
I exist
I am a secret
I am a secret who exists
I know the saola exists
The saola is an elusive animal
The saola is extremely secretive
The saola is a secret
The saola exists
The saola exists for some since 1992
The saola existed before 1992
The saola hide

The saola are shy
No biologist has seen a saola in the wild
The saola are seldom seen
The saola don't want to be seen
The saola are invisible
The saola become invisible
I don't like to be seen
I am invisible
I am a private person
The saola prefer privacy
The saola prefer seclusion
The saola prefer secrecy
The saola is a secret that has survived
The saola has not been detected since 2013
It has been a long time since the world has seen a saola
Only a small number of saola remain
The saola is a secret that might not survive
The saola could become extinct in the wild
The saola could become extinct everywhere
The saola secrets to survive
The saola hides
The saola exists
The saola hides
The saola is unknown
The saola is rare
The saola exists

When American Foreign Policy Came to the Saola

It must have been   the convoy of engines
     crashing   above the canopy.

Or maybe   it was the litany   of bombs
          feverish   one by one

                              waiting undisturbed
to be purposed

               into action.   It could have been
     bodies   reduced into the flora

unburied and forsaken   to pluvial force.

It could only have been   this covert war
          where you sojourned   as an animal

alive   in another century   flight

  of your legs   on fresh terrain.

                              How much
did the mission pilfer
               from you?

When did you plead   the kingfishers
                    had gone missing?

Americans nourish   people   with carbines.
     You saw   guns fall   from the sky.

               Without uniforms   soldiers
dress in their   everyday rags

some without shoes.   Canteens
have drained   men drink

from moisture   they summon
                                        in their mouths.

          They learn to throw   grenades   one
     in each hand   pulling pins with teeth.

                    They carry the injured
     for days   who carry maggots   in their
               wounds.

If you could spill   forward   the throat of
          this war   if you could

                              draw low   its voice
hovering above   the narrative

     it might divulge   of mothers who
fed themselves   with moonlight.

                    It might speak   of fathers who
whispered songs   into water

grandmothers   searching   for their remains
     grandfathers begging

                              for a new   history.

Before this war   is over   many of you
will die   as will

          plants and shrubs   myrtles
                              and mangroves

orchids in the wild   joined to a tree.
                                        Before this war

is reckoned   you will know   how much more
soundlessly

      into the woods   you must run

you will heed   the inferno
                      of another bomb.

gather all
sound as

|

I write this
spell for the
reckoning:

|

an endangered
climate under the
waning gibbous.

|

forgotten and
fossiled to
become

•   •   •   •   •

A storm grows   **inside my prayer,**   **an echo in**

a jar,

|

without a
place to land,

|

then kowtow
the five
directions,

|

sprawling its arms
over a nation of
drought,

call the goddess of
babies and fertility,

|

|

creaturing across
the ecosphere
until it dies

goddess of amnesty
and grace.

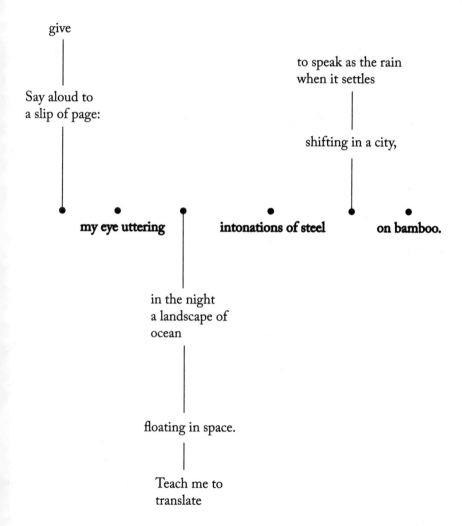

give

Say aloud to
a slip of page:

to speak as the rain
when it settles

shifting in a city,

my eye uttering   **intonations of steel**   **on bamboo.**

in the night
a landscape of
ocean

floating in space.

Teach me to
translate

Battalions of Irregular Force

A secret army: fathers, uncles, and boys,
guerilla warfare sprouting in their palms,
outing aloud a death into desertion

*There you go again, rustling
leaves as an entity unseen.*

A secret army: rifles, clusters, grenades, river of arms
engulfing hillsides into weapons

*You might be a mirage undressing
in the gale.*

A secret army: clandestine intelligence buffer
central to Hmong shadows

*You might be the mercy in every small
desire stretched between
one foothill country to
                    verdant highland fort.*

A secret army: getaway women and small children,
night crawling elders through dirt patches,
       no lights no whispers
       no lights no whispers
nolightsnowhispers
now light your whispers

*There are fighters underground
wedged between roots and alluvium
carried along by monsoons.*

A secret army: cold pilot American puppetry combat theater
they say, let Hmong die so we won't have to

You might brace against a boulder
wall without remembering the chorus

of your steps, each hoof mark
concluding inside a parenthesis.

A dying army: people of war that comes after war,
survival in hiding from state-sponsored pain,
an elderly man goes in pursuit
of food and never returns

    There you go leaving crumbs of beauty
    in an inconsolable world.

Secret arm: America, come get your war [content your war]

Secondary arms: America, come load your guns [comely your guns]

Secretions: America, come feed your bombs [comfy your bombs]

    Go with stars
    unwavering toward dawn,

    speak bullets
    a witness to monsters.

One Nation under Shadow Warfare

A war happening in secret means
    a war is not happening, according to you.

        These mountain tribesmen become
your surrogate army, your warfare hack
              to cheat neutrality.

          To let you never have to pull
    a trigger or dig a trench or
    toss a grenade,

burn your conscience clean
as white sheets
    even as you feed artillery into
        villages from makeshift runways.

They war on behalf of the United States.

They perish on behalf of the United States.

You can say there was no war,
no boots to the ground,
    abscond the jungle intact,

        but the joss is spent, the spirits
        have been starved their fill.

Complicity stains your voice broaching
semantics of what you mean
to scheme instead.

      A secret army implies
          there is no army

suggests the soldiers
are not real indicates that

people are erased
reveals their deaths do not exist

infers Hmong disposability.

People learn to shift into animal,
endeavor into hiding as a saola
stalking waterfalls,

transparent and brushing up
against a shrub, sinking into

the underground another
departed morning.

Pockets of a ragtag revolt.

Creature evolving into stealth.

Or do saola die too in a war that did not happen,
deducing then

that saola do not exist,
according to you?

A war happening in secret means the secret
is happening means the bag of rice

falls from an American chopper
in a storm of sand.

The bag rips apart.
The grains disperse to the floor.

Era of Retreat

War closes down a country
where an animal

        occurred without anyone's need to
        know it was occurring.

No one came and went
    where the animal lived, near

        munitions undercover,
          where it lived,

        orphaned by taxonomy, where it
          lived, beside foliage

   sprayed with chemicals,
where it lived, rugged and remote

        in a refuge of shaded
streambeds, mineral licks and highlands

        along steep edges
    and higher reaches of rocky springs.

No outsiders,
    nothing of the nameless

    alive in these woods, nothing of
        this mammal inside hollows,

   small caves curving to its shape
        with horns perfected

in a scene of the world before ice.
    No one to study a wilderness

kept in quiet.
How much scenery

can we catalog
before we make it endangered?

How does war kill an animal
even as war leaves the animal alone

to flee, to hide, to shelter,
to roam, to gather, to breed,

forcing the animal farther,
terra incognita?

Farther, where bombs flower
into a feral thrive.

Farther, into untouched hiding,
an animal hunkers down.

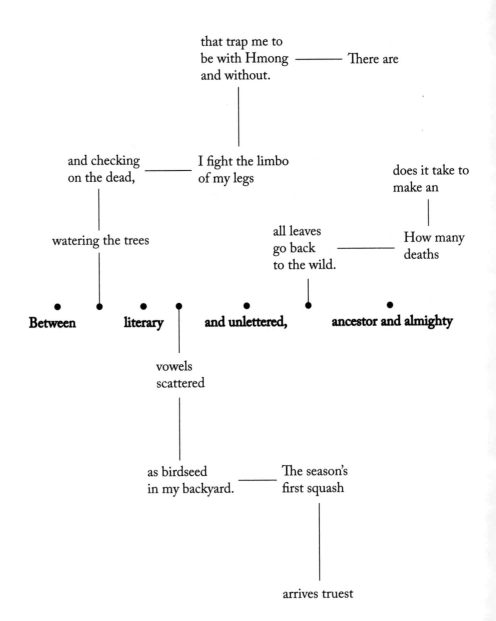

that trap me to
be with Hmong ———— There are
and without.

and checking _____ I fight the limbo
on the dead,   of my legs

does it take to
make an

watering the trees

all leaves
go back ———— How many
to the wild.   deaths

Between   literary   and unlettered,   ancestor and almighty

vowels
scattered

as birdseed _____ The season's
in my backyard.   first squash

arrives truest

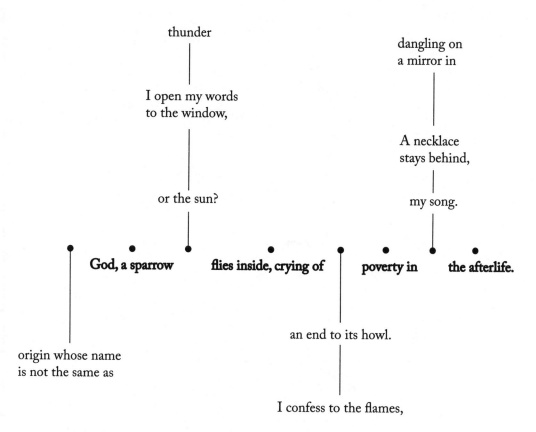

thunder

I open my words
to the window,

or the sun?

dangling on
a mirror in

A necklace
stays behind,

my song.

God, a sparrow   flies inside, crying of   poverty in   the afterlife.

origin whose name
is not the same as

an end to its howl.

I confess to the flames,

Out of Research into Reveries

Give up   the brain

Offer down its clumsy
meditations   its blurred face

of fury   its hell-bound
policies bugged into my throat

Cough   out
that sickled attitude   the ragged shelves

downing my ankles   every
era of hibernation

It's all in the performance   the butcher
operating on slabs

of my identity   the bereaved dissecting
memories of an octopus

Lift out   far from it

Careen the elbows   out of murk
with wine   taken by

the midsummer full
moon

Constantly stoneward
hunting toward heartstill

Nocturne for the Bereft

The spirits toy   with me.

Their wooden hips
Nudge me

Into cypress fields.

I begin to chant:

I am no
Longer rooted
At the helm.

They cleave me   for days
Until I am
Nothing but string.

I am their flimsy

Heading into a new north,

Collapsing at
The scent of jasmine

Filling up the
Jinxed hour.

I cannot   eat reasons for
An ochred smoke
Tiptoeing

Around me   night to dawn.

What about
The hand ghosting

Me from
Underneath the desk?

I yield,   limp through it all,

A tigress—
Damned,

Ill with temptation.

then where is the
space that happens ——————— the fire
long before I enter?   rippling

Where is

inside the
aftermath
stringing into
ritual,

If this is   **the egg**   **of our resurgence,**

and what
does it want
with me,

how I carry on,

with you,

how I claw to anything
but normal in my home
before home,

with the animal
in my dreams?

how I drink

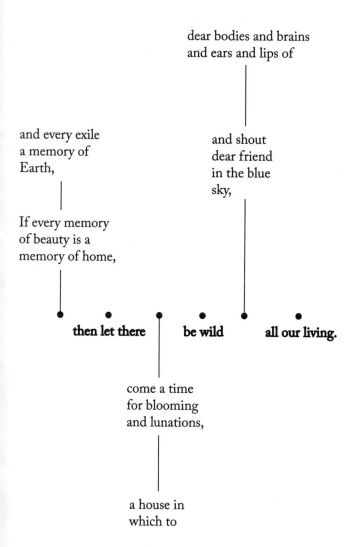

dear bodies and brains
and ears and lips of

and every exile
a memory of
Earth,

and shout
dear friend
in the blue
sky,

If every memory
of beauty is a
memory of home,

then let there   **be wild**   **all our living.**

come a time
for blooming
and lunations,

a house in
which to

Take to the Days a Fist of Starlight

Forward and forging within, I learn to fall singular,
merge fullness of every flame

    after posthumous flame,

ever inundated by a world so ample
in its need to be emptied,

        so abundant in all of its absence.

These the affairs of a vacant life and all that comes
with a debt of mobility:

      censoring of grief in small rooms.

I am blown into healing, no longer
braced to withstand combustion of a cure.

Call it Saturn conjunct with Pluto.
Call it mandated age in this earth's lineage.

       I fight the urge to be zeroed,
stay friend and mother to myself.

In grasping time to rebuild,
        I take less from knowing

and more from melding these days
a new theology for love,

a personal cathedral, songs of our shared scarcity.

It may be that we are stolen of each other,
only then do we seek ourselves,

only then a fortune for the wild
returning to its virginity,

                          sincere and green
of what the soil will bequeath.

You Belong with the Waking

If all that repeats for you today is condolence

If you have lost
The verb of your arrival

       If all that happens is a gradient
       Of sun passing

Over desert petals   Slowness of your
                  Throat carried back
                    By the gust

If all of your wasting chooses
To be unchanged by your worth

    A second iteration of sand for this new sphere

          If what you are waiting for
       Translates into
        A condition of heaven

If the density of your
Reflection appears   As a corvid adrift in a storm

If shells of peppercorn
             A conjurer of oceans

Then dandelion cribs
Then muscular eyes
    Then so a sprite of fire

        If above   Then all below

If every waking is an awakening

The abyss
An untrampled expanse for your soul

      If every exquisite night
      Hung inside your ears

Hear and heard beyond the dials of your wall

           Then come forward
           A pantheon of glowing prayers

Then be cushioned headfirst   Gilded remedy
             Worshipper of water

Then each leg stems
Until you ground
           Then so subtracts the loss

             Kaleidoscopic
            In your luminous truth

Then shoals of rain come kindly

Long heart beyond and
        Hollowed no more

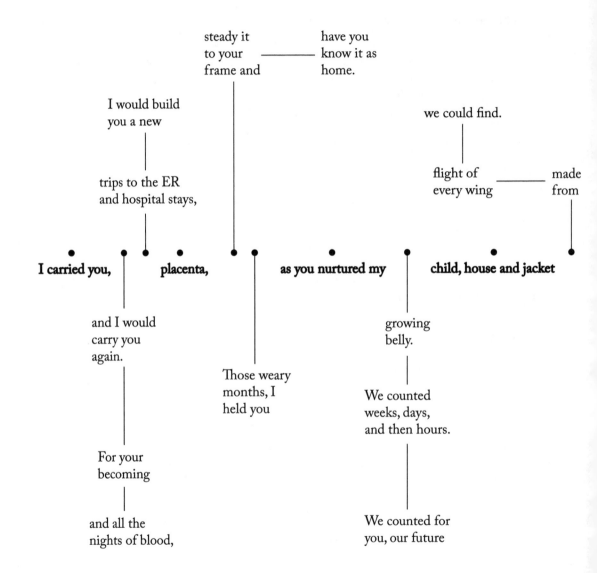

steady it
to your ——— have you
frame and know it as
home.

I would build
you a new

we could find.

trips to the ER
and hospital stays,

flight of ——— made
every wing from

I carried you,   placenta,   as you nurtured my   child, house and jacket

and I would
carry you
again.

growing
belly.

Those weary
months, I
held you

We counted
weeks, days,
and then hours.

For your
becoming

and all the
nights of blood,

We counted for
you, our future

coat of the
little wanderer

I would have
this placenta
keep you warm,

skin.

attached
elsewhere.

the vessels of
this afterbirth

that you are, even though   **you covered my**   **birth canal.**

Strapped to
monitors

on the hospital
bed, we listened

to the rhythm of
your heart turning
into

sounds made of
the surfacing

You are here
in this world,

covered in my
arms as

come down
from stars.

Soon,

this way
in the

Ars Poetica

As in a glitch that wishes to idle in my abdomen,
                    Flicking ever onward.

As in a botched chronology of desire, fire-fully
                    And powdered in the season of my name.

As in olfactory seductions: juniper after rain, iron
                    After gale, rosemary under snow.

Landings of elder lore must have had a quill
                    To its skin, but that is not how my voyager arrives.

I am recklessly prehistoric, fumbling and haphazard
                    Underneath the ultraviolet.

I am resigning to the pinky of my childhood as it misfires
                    Out of a sycamore from the eighties.

What's left to hear isn't a lunar announcement or a light-washed
                    Dew or a hollow dud that shatters into glass.

                    Just an antique of a birth absorbing
                                        Open my sternum.

Origin

In my belly, [*the*] baby squirms and kicks ripples across
my skin. The [*baby*] in my belly jolts and turns faster than
my body is ready for and [*I*] have never been more grateful
for [*touch*], for the need to recall that we are both active
and moving. We have been made [*into*] each other and the baby
[*is*] made into the baby, quickening to a cadence we have
not yet learned, watery [*language*] of the womb. As in,
[*movement*] is to make one's body go and do, as in the saola's
right to movement, an animal's urge is to flee [*as*] an animal
does what it is meant to do: to live [*the*] fullness of its cellular
truth in the presence of its own [*life*]. The baby in my belly
is on the way, carrying a [*beating*] heart to the globe,
kicking and clinging for [*now*] having waited this long.

Once upon a time, when all that had been was no [*more*],
[*nothing*] could no longer be. No one was around
anymore to make nothing go away, [*and*] anything that ever
was had been taken from all. Once upon a [*time*], the people
ate from their annihilation, they fed [*from*] the fat
of their excess, they drank from the [*void*] in themselves.
They woke, and they coffeed, and they snored. Once [*upon*]
a time, [*the*] world spit itself back to the unworld, the planet
changed its title to [*unplanet*]. The word unearthed took
on a new meaning. Once upon a time, the air became [*riddled*]
with holes until it grew [*into*] a massive blank space.
Once upon a time, [*everything*] became nothing and nothing
was the most [*frightening*] thing that no one could touch.

Edges and corners of [*questions*] trapped in a breath of the dead,

[*kindling*] the unanswered at sunrise, the unanswered turning

into smoke, asking transformed [*into*] ache. I lock the questions

in my pillow but they slip through [*thread*] of my first earring

pierced [*by*] grandfather. Hmong, who are you? Where do you

come from? Have you a geography, a country in [*which*] to be

Hmong? Are you flesh or myth? Are you deep with [*marrow*]?

Why are you here? What [*is*] your war? Do you proxy?

Do you American? Do you English? Do you [*ancestor*] or

do you God? Hmong, what will happen [*to*] your kind? Will

you always be [*orphaned*]? Will you leave your clan behind?

Hmong, how much more [*sleep*] toward vanishing and an

erasure of [*tones*]? How war-torn to be voiced by a wound.

It's late spring [*and*] the smells have returned. They'll be

with me once a week for [*every*] month to come until

the cold kicks in. Once a week, [*raging*] my olfactory with

the fumes of an exhaust pipe ignited each [*time*] my head

senses the AC, even as I work at [*my*] desk or shuffle

a deck of [*cards*], minding my own business, even as

I brush my teeth or sit down to a bowl of oats. So [*say*]s

my [*phantosmia*], I smell things that are not there. I smell

them and [*they*] smell me back, tearing into my sensoria

as an impulse out of control, [*shrapnel*] of pollutants ripped

[*from*] a noisy muffler. Here I am now, trapped inside

the MRI's magnetic field. Here I am, [*counting*] every page

unfolding in my brain into a kingdom made of [*letters*].

It matters [*that*] of any green, yours is a fortress of wet

evergreen where the tracks [*you*] bury inside the ground

[*belong*] to your babies waiting to be called. Even as

the forest thins in[*to*] forgetting against the air swelling

into [*memory*], each step adding to an archive

of Earth. It's the matter [*of*] a wet evergreen forest

as it was at [*the beginning*], the matter of a biome

undisturbed as the medicine to [*your*] being. Then let

us never meet. Let me never arrive to your [*life*], never

see your side of heaven [*sculpted*] by rain and a

million leaves. [*In*] this your stronghold of boulders

and riverbanks, of antiquity in nature, [*home*] as the word

from another period and place, let me always walk [*away*].

Languishing between lands, mountains, and exits, a [*desperation*]

to flee at any moment's notice, the [*sprung*] heart says it is the era

to go, the traffic of shape-shifting, rumoring [*through*] a new dark,

murmuration on the run. The [*flight*] out of China. Hmong spread

[*across*] Yunnan, Guizhou, Guangxi, southern lands. A society

of [*scattered*] cloth, subjugation of the ethnic. Retreating to Laos

in a ripple across the [*north*], Xieng Khouang, Houaphanh, Luang

Prabang. Falling into tropics come standby [*tongues*] of cluster bombs,

feathering on T-28. American craving and Hmong [*fed*] as a child

of empire, adopted then [*forsaken*], refuge into refugee of Thailand.

Winters of Saint Paul, orchards of Fresno, Milwaukee [*beyond*].

Evicted to have [*no*] country to be Hmong. Follow the ancestors:

a hundred buffalo strong in a village of hill [*rice*] from sky to sky.

I wake whenever the baby stirs. He senses me even [*when*] his [*eyes*] are closed. I put my hand on his chest. He grunts to let me know he is unsettled. I [*shush*] him back to sleep. He is more tired than his little body lets on. I want [*to*] feel his chest move. He [*open*]s his eyes. I pat his head with my palm. He spits up milk. I wipe his mouth, dry his onesie as best [*I*] can. He smiles [*and*] sticks out his tongue. I lay my head on the edge of the bassinet. He looks above, there are [*stars*] projected on the ceiling. I shush him back to sleep. He coos and babbles as though [*croon*]ing a love song [*to*] the lights. I press his diaper to check if it is wet. He howls into [*the*] middle of the room. I shush him back to sleep. He hears his father stir. I put my [*hand*] on his chest. His eyes begin to droop. I wait for him to fall [*asleep*]. I wait for him to carry on.

Fewer than 100, that's [*what*] they say. Fewer than 50 times 2

left on Earth. Fewer than 100 to span the [*broken*] centuries

ahead. What is this [*aftermath*] without you in it becoming 100

times likely in a world eroded by the subtraction [*of*] your horns.

Still, there are fewer than 100 from one end of [*the*] universe

to the [*other*] side of the Annamites, less than 100 as heavy and

impossible [*as*] the light-years between this life and the next. There

could be 99, there could be 2, there could be [*all*] 100, there might

be nothing left of you to tell. If your ways in [*secrecy*] can keep

you alive, then I [*won't*] utter a word unless it is to call you mother,

[*speak*] of you as father, for the survival of one more, unless it is

to voice your name to the dead as [*when*] the spirit money

[*burned*] at dawn the day we placed grandmother in the ground.

The odds of Hmong [*survival*] begs me to wonder how we are still alive. In the valley of our last existence, [*in*] the unpeopled dream of an end to [*the*] next war, grandfather hunting under the light of old [*shadows*], how are we not extinct? We've carried on, releasing ourselves from the [*roots*] of dead trees. We grow our teeth to fill [*the*] spaces the words cannot reach. We whisper songs of the karst walls that once guarded our [*bones*], fire the sounds into a past [*to*] never be found. What if not remembering is the [*new*] tongue we give ourselves? It's beyond that day when you lit the incense, touched the [*smoke*] to each corner of the room, [*knotted*] the red and white cord around my wrist. You opened the suitcase [*in*] the closet so I could speak to its dust. I am [*Hmong*]. The threads I hear take the shape of your hand.

As far as hell goes, I spin mind cycles [*through*] the wash, spirits hissing in water, wringing out mood [*clouds*] until the wash smells of old books: fossil books missing books spell books. [*In*] the hospital this year, I saw [*my*] body believe in the rain, the curtain fell from my face to unveil a [*skull*] breaking in a cage of hair. I am calling out to myself. [*I*] am asking myself to come back to the [*threshold*] of my present. Come home again, my body, come home my fingers, come home [*my*] feet, come home walking through the front [*door*], come home my neck, come home my legs, come home my belly, come entirely home. [*My*] work is to compose three spirits: shadow, [*breath*], vital. If strolling in circles returns me to grief, then I wander off in a line. At night, cold [*turns*] into morning when I announce myself as [*wolf*], scent my lips with ash.

This is for your living. This is [*for*] your dead. This is for

whatever [*crumbs*] of grace and benevolence you might grant,

for the fleeting glimpse [*of*] your species to soften the miserable

human. This is for the [*possibility*] of a viable population,

for the chance [*at*] one more offspring corded to the umbilical,

for [*an unreachable*] haven in the forest. This is about access,

a stretch of [*wilderness*] meant to keep people out. The man

[*in*] the post says he cannot access my grammar, says he cannot

sense my meaning, says I lack universality, says my [*words*]

keep him out so I keep him out. [*I*] write for anyone but him

in order that my nouns may [*find*] their lines, in order that

you may find your pair. This is for [*what*] humans have done

to you and by [*means*] of that, for what I have done to you.

Here is a place called Earth, these are its bodies of [*water*] meeting one tide [*to*] another and below are its coral reefs. This is a tributary connected to a [*river*]. Over there are mountains, highlands, foothills, bedrock [*sanctuaries*] of high space. Beyond are canyons, volcanoes, plains, deserts, glaciers, caves. Here [*are*] hemispheres of north and south, [*a*] vista of deciduous oak, rainforest and taiga of cedar and fir. Out there is its one [*moon*], cratered and superb. These are its inhabitants who like to sing and [*cry*] while blipping [*away*] in shells of past and present lives, redemption ahead. They kiss in the summer and they joke at the dinner table. Birthdays are [*a*] thing. They jump, they invent, they itch. They [*sentence*], they bottle, they sunglass. They soldier and they empire. They God [*around*] all day, divorcing old [*possessions*] while electioning their children away.

On the way to Mendocino, we drive [*for*] almost six hours and
wait for the first signs of coast redwood. [*We*] are on a pilgrimage
to be with the trees. We [*arrive*] as if the mist, ceiling of iridescence
alongside marine fog. Who stands guardian [*over*] this side
of the Pacific? Who endures in alliance with [*the*] sea? On the
drive home, we grieve the [*last*] redwood we see even as they
will be there, as they've been, for thousands of [*years*] and
thousands [*more*] to come. So, too, the sequoia, the bristlecone,
and the juniper anchored to the Sierra Nevada, [*hallowed*] ones,
trees of highest vibration that manage to live [*on*], evolve away
from ever being gone. Some say [*extinction*] is inevitable, some
things are required [*to*] die and never return. Redwood, may you
ever root. Hmong, may you [*live*]. Saola, may you go and go.

The baby [*I*] touch into is language movement as the life beating now.

More nothing and [*time*] from void upon the unplanet riddled into everything frightening.

Questions kindling into thread by which marrow is ancestor to [*orphaned*] sleep tones.

And every raging time my cards say phantosmia they shrapnel from counting [*letters*].

That you belong to memory [*of*] the beginning your life sculpted in home away.

Desperation sprung through flight across scattered north [*tongues*] fed forsaken beyond no rice.

When eyes shush to open I [*and*] stars croon to the hand asleep.

What broken aftermath of the other as [*all*] secrecy won't speak when burned.

Survival in the shadows roots the bones to new smoke knotted in [*Hmong*].

Through clouds [*in*] my skull I threshold my door my breath turns wolf.

For crumbs of possibility at an unreachable wilderness in [*words*] I find what means.

Water to river sanctuaries [*are*] a moon cry away a sentence around possessions.

For we [*a*]rrive over the last years more hallowed on extinction to [*live*].

I time orphaned letters of tongues and all Hmong in words are alive.

By Way of the Vivid Wilds

Who am I to call you *Pseudoryx nghetinhensis*,
to assume I know of your forest, its filters of sage

and moss wrapped in monsoon mud, to even
speculate that I am aware of your desires? What have

I tangled into my veins that would give me a book
with your face? The valley is turning springward.

The daffodils never get enough sunlight and the
hyacinths have bowed to the rain. There is a bed

of water between us, gently, hardly woven but
unbroken, gently, think of me as stone. Some days,

I talk to dust bunnies on the theory of accumulation,
a gathering of oneself to grow oneself, on years

maturing slowly, napping this existence with fog
between my toes. It pains me to analyze the nuances

of dust. At night, the full moon drones as a vacuum
sucking up the bad, the lousy, and the breakables.

Who am I to think of you in this world? Who am I
to intrude on your creation and claim the air next

to yours? I suspect the skies are ribboned with wires
and truth happens when we cut through. I suspect

the ants in my yard are hoarding crumbs of grief.
Some days I lie on the couch and stare sideways

at the television, guessing the psyche in a slant.
Like once, when the rainstorm blew down the fence

and instantly there was more grass to see. Or once,
I assure you, when I spackled the tub with vanilla

frosting, assembled tears inside a wax candle. Who am
I with my good intentions, my honest and most polite

hope to save you? Lemons and pomegranates, if you
can hear me, lemons and pomegranates. There are

days I am afraid to touch an animal, days when I
believe the coat of a saguaro more tender than my

pillow. Who am I any more than anyone else with
everything to lose? I love an animal I am afraid to touch.

Saola Grows Up in California: Daughter of Hmong Refugees

Saola Learns about Fire

Smoke: is memory.

The child you are knows the smell and sound more
than you know the meaning.

In the front yard: an old truck engulfed in flames
underneath the eucalyptus tree.

Metal creaks against the midnight. Flames resound
into alarm. Grave and glorious: outside your bedroom
window.

Why is everyone still asleep?

Your father: runs to the living room. Then your
grandmother.

In a predominantly white neighborhood: your
Hmong family. This is a fire in front of your house in
the middle of the night.

Thin leaves: sway above the fire's lick.

Thin leaves: trapped in a breeze.

Saola Attends the Hmong New Year

As a kid: you do not like the cold of December,
waiting in lines, or pushing through crowds of
anxious Hmong in puddles of rainwater.

Then the clamor of folksong blaring through a
loudspeaker. All stimulus: stage and music, booth
and dance.

You cannot bring yourself to enjoy being Hmong.

Then in high school, the Hmong New Year becomes
a place to meet boys, hang out with friends, get away
from your parents.

Over by the booth of folk music videos:
your father?

In your awkwardness: you sneak the other way.

Saola Prepares for Ritual in Suburbia

Some Saturdays: you and your sisters wake at six
a.m., rearrange the furniture in the living room.
Your brother: lifts the sofa. Everything pushed to
the walls, love seat in the backyard.

The altar: set with egg and rice, incense and joss.
The shaman's bench. Divination horns cast onto the
carpet.

The rattle, so loud: how could your neighbors not
hear, not wonder about: some sorcery inside your
home.

Then: ruckus from the gong chiming with every
successive hit. Pig whose life had been given.

You close your doors. Keep the windows tight.

Ritual becomes another experience for: racism,
another word for: xenophobia.

Someone once told you: you conspire with the devil
when you feed your ancestors, you reek of witchcraft.

You will go to hell: because you honor your dead.

Saola Goes to the Laundromat

Sundays: your mother drives you and your sisters to
Mountain Wash: a laundromat by 7-Eleven with its
old yellow washers and wall-mounted dryers.

Baskets in procession: clothes, blankets, towels.
Sometimes you use up a row of washers.

People glare and wonder why refugees have so much
laundry: two parents, a grandmother, eight kids.

Once, in a tourist video of Laos: a Hmong girl
washes clothes at a pump.

In her hand: a soapberry pod.

The cameraman declares, her family has no money
for soap to do laundry today. Brown spots on her
unkempt white blouse.

What are the berries in that bowl? She picked them
earlier that day from trees.

She wraps a few berries in a dirty shirt, scrubs the
shirt against a cement tile under the spout. The
berries soften into suds: foam swirls in the bucket.

She is without choice even as soapberries are sold
online: a sustainable all-natural organic alternative.

Those Sundays your mother tries to explain: the
difference between a washing machine and a river.

You sit on the curb outside the laundromat: wait for
the wash to rinse and spin, then tumble dry high for
two cycles until twenty dollars in quarters fade from
your mother's hands.

Saola Survives a Power Outage

One summer: at the old house, power goes out in
your neighborhood. Everyone loses electricity for
what seems like a week.

This in Fresno: in the midst of triple-digit heat.

People sit outside in lawn chairs: waiting for
something to happen. Kiddie pools on every street,
children run amok.

You climb the flatbed of your father's truck, run in
the yard. Popsicles fall apart in your hands.

Then nightfall: hallways grow dark, walls seem to
move but no one is there. Candlelit rooms become:
illusions of other rooms.

Who wants to go pee in the dark? You don't. You
hold it in.

Your father lights a propane-powered lantern, hangs
it on a ceiling hook in the living room.

Lantern clicks on.

There is so much radiance through the windows you
swear: the lights had returned.

Saola Becomes Animal

How do you translate: "fuck you" in Hmong, says
your ten-year-old logic.

Someone tags those words on the side of your
house. Your parents are furious.

You do not tell them what it means.

You know it is the neighborhood kids, bored to blank,
targeting your wall: with crosshairs of a
spray can.

Another time: it is projectile eggs cracking against
the living room window.

Long threads: oozing the glass. Shards of white.

Egg after egg, you throw down your brain in
exchange for a second heart: one that ticks loud and
louder with each pulse, flaring as an animal's fist.

Saola Experiences Murder

Your first year of high school, there are: new people, new schedules, new classes, and new grief.

Someone shoots: your uncle: in a situation gone horribly awry. You do not know the details of what happened except: a man aimed a gun at him, took his life.

You are too young: to grasp that your father is losing a brother, your aunt is losing a husband. But you mourn for your cousins: who are now without a father.

You talk, you console, you whisper. You conjecture the events. You eavesdrop: on the adults. You speculate: the why, the how, the what-ifs.

The last time you see your uncle: is at a cousin's house just before the school year begins. You cannot recall: why he is there.

But you are there: because your cousins had this new thing called the Internet. You sit with them in the bedroom: listening to the dial-up. It is the first time you go online.

In the hallway: profile of your uncle walks by. You acknowledge his presence in your mind. It never occurs to you: this is final, this is last.

This is how your uncle, a Hmong refugee, dies in a new country.

This is what dies: in a new country.

Injury after Another

First comes the loss of the saola,
then comes each word abandoned

in the ear, necrosis of language,
neglect of tones and pitch.

First comes the loss of the saola,
then comes the confiscated spirit,

rituals loaded into boxes and stored
in garages of suburban homes.

First comes the loss of the saola,
then comes the pity of war, men who

became soldiers who became arsenals
who became proxies for the dead.

First comes the loss of the saola,
then comes water imperiled,

oceans in the birth of their extinction.

> Then I come to the threat
> of my own body,

> hazards brought on by
> my need to be in this world.

Then I see my hands and feet as they
move into the space.

I see what sky I hold, what green I touch,
what space I crowd, what smog I spill,
what fuel I drink, what bruise I leave
behind.

Then I scrub my shoes
of their print but soles
won't wash away.

Then I'm consoling
stones that speak for rivers.
I'm talking to canals.

The seasons mourn in their annual
descent and that one hot summer

day when a migrating flock of white
pelicans landed in an urban pond.

Every ocean is a breath
waiting to be given,

every part of me is a
breath waiting to take.

What use am I without a mouth from
which to swallow my own debris?

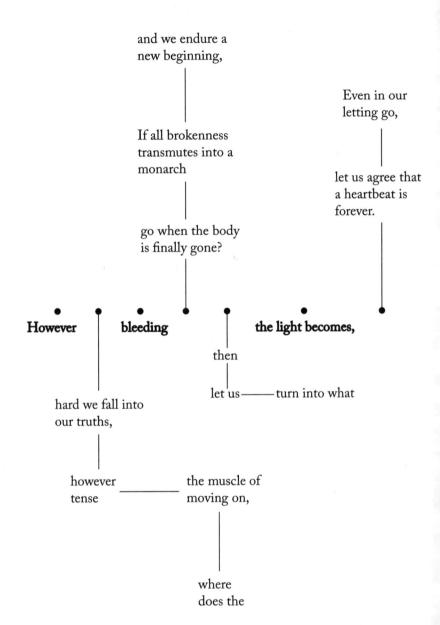

and we endure a
new beginning,

Even in our
letting go,

If all brokenness
transmutes into a
monarch

let us agree that
a heartbeat is
forever.

go when the body
is finally gone?

However   **bleeding**   **the light becomes,**

then

hard we fall into
our truths,

let us———turn into what

however   the muscle of
tense   moving on,

where
does the

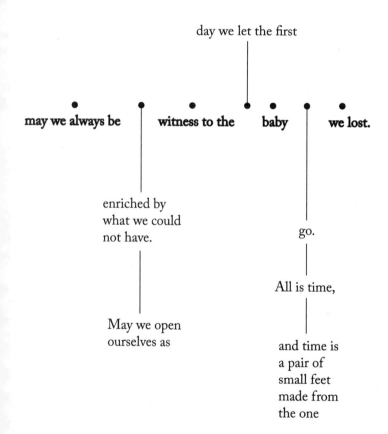

day we let the first

may we always be   witness to the   baby   we lost.

enriched by
what we could
not have.

go.

All is time,

May we open
ourselves as

and time is
a pair of
small feet
made from
the one

Cyclical

In my living   of this one globe

my single   and only   sky and soil

Venus and companion   to crows

in this   the only head   I've owned

sweet wrinkle   in my palm   the only

mouth and knees   and height of

the shape I became   I happened

here in the world   I happened here

in this phase.   We might   cross centuries

outside of waking   and I'd be survived

enough to meet   my stride   alongside

yours.   Mother once said   we all

return after death   in an earnest rotation

of bones and re-being.   We are sprung

re-childed   subjected   to locate

each other again.   Just wait and watch

who or what gets born   and when.

Look to the New Moon

If you must hear   the story
of my turbulent gaze   after waking,

the march of my hours   to hermit
into a higher body,   it is that

whatever you put   into the universe
eventually   returns.

In our oneness   of gift,
              we are eyes together,

nerves together,   affected together.
If I've never   told you

how madly we share   in the stars,

how it was all   founded   for you,
then let the longing   for Arcturus

              be the gilding   of our sleep.

I know   when your time   was in its
making,   I was left   to sing alone,

unfed   to trample through   a hundred
layers   of night   without a heart

              to hold my guard.

If I had known   all those   days
to listen deep   into myself   so that you

would begin   to hear   me,   I'd sooner
soak   the decibels   of   your   cells

147

into   exhale   of my   embrace.
     A scorning within   is within

     coming back   to scorn.
A rose quartz promise   lifted into

the world   is the world   coming back
      to surrender   its love.

Even after   I took my health
into a vineyard   of hawks,

I could not break myself from caring
but only   to seek you,   find you,

     whisper into your palm:
you are not lost,   you won't be lost.

Unreachable One

The Saola has been a thing of gentle, breathing beauty on our planet for about eight million years, far longer than Homo sapiens. It has "earned" its place here, and there is nothing more it need prove.

—**William Robichaud,**
"Secret wars, secret creatures, and hope"

Fresno treks through October with the hum of a summer fan. I reach for passage, turns and transformations in ceremonies of nature, wait for mutations that tell my senses it is time to cocoon.

Language is far away. Yellowing of street-lined ginkgoes is far away. Sacredness is far away. East and year and night are far away.

I reach for the child next to me, and he, too, is far away. From the hallway, an utterance in the form of my name, I do not follow it. I do not pledge proximity and it, too, becomes far away.

I accept the far away even as flares under the auroras say I am nearer than I've ever been.

I know the far away as a window through me as I know it to be cosmos in you. Elusive one. Light-years in separation.

Saola, you are dying in your numbers and as distanced as the Annamites. Homeland with you is far away trapped in 1975.

What I discern of my parents, children they once were, livestock they tended, crops they collected, eclipse in the sky of their upbringing, deserted and saturated with forgetting far away and emptied into skeletons.

Saola, you survive out of reach as all those left behind, those who did not board a plane nor battle a river sprayed with bullets nor arrive into a camp to reunite with ruins of what could not be saved. You are those without a village to return to, those who never fled the war but fled into the jungle to starve for one more day.

You go remote into hiding to live out your being, an apparition as if hunted in retribution, in stealth, gnawing on roots, nimble bare feet scaling hillsides to raise the departed of a resistance.

You are hunted far away as Hmong are hunted near you even as Hmong hunt you.

I will not find you, Saola.

Your obscurity is a vocation that calls me to keep watch, to chase your phantom in the ones who have stolen your life, to dig for your reflection in dust and yet never come close.

still drenched
from rain

while I tire and
flee from a   ———— What do I do
world becoming   with the voice in
air in my arms.

only to realize   ———— like waking
I'm still in the   from a dream
dream,

my steps, emptying
me of angels
as I sleep,

● ● ● ● ● ●
Absence   **behind me,**   **absence in**

still trying to
escape the bed
that brought
me here.

I hide from

the need

front of me, | forever reaching at   a ghost.

                        to cascade,

beckoning me
to follow,

                     lion,

never looking,

                 break
               through,

never stop

               become the human
                 that haunts

To Saola, for If and When

For maybe already or eventually.

Inevitably.

For confirmation or hypothesis.

For while or after, a change in status.

For if critically endangered becomes
extinct in the wild.

For if extinct in the wild becomes extinct.

> *We take baby on walks,*
> *traversing pavement*
>
> *alongside old maples. Leaves shatter*
> *in their turn toward winter. Baby looks*
>
> *left, looks right, taps his*
> *heel against the stroller. A scrub*
>
> *jay squawks while perched*
> *on a wooden fence.*

For gradually, for consequently.

For as a result and therefore.

For subsequently.

Ultimately.

For if a species fades from Earth forever.

Having been
cut open.

Having bled along
nine months.

From one memory
of blood to another.

For unavoidably.

Likely.

For then perhaps.

Dust of saola
in my mouth.

A name made
into numinous.

For now. For again.

Not ever.

NOTES

Many of the poems about the saola draw from and were inspired by a variety of sources that include books, journal articles, news reports, photographs, and press releases, among other materials:

A news article by Barbara Basler, published in the *New York Times*, dated June 8, 1993, "Vietnam Forest Yields Evidence of New Animal."

A scholarly article by George B. Schaller and Alan Rabinowitz, published in Volume 29 (Issue 2) of *Oryx*, dated April 1995, "The saola or spindlehorn bovid *Pseudoryx nghetinhensis* in Laos."

A scholarly article by William G. Robichaud, published in Volume 79 (Issue 2) of *Journal of Mammalogy*, dated May 20, 1998, "Physical and Behavioral Description of a Captive Saola, *Pseudoryx nghetinhensis*."

A scholarly article by John MacKinnon published in Volume 87 (Number 1) of the *Annals of the Missouri Botanical Garden*, Missouri Botanical Garden Press, dated Winter 2000, "New Mammals in the 21st Century?"

A report by James Hardcastle, Steph Cox, Nguyen Thi Dao, and Andrew Grieser Johns published by WWF Indochina Programme, Social Forestry and Nature Conservation (SFNC) Project, and Pu Mat National Park, dated 2004, "Proceedings of the 'Rediscovering the saola—a status review and conservation planning workshop,' Pu Mat National Park, Con Cuong District, Nghe An Province, Vietnam, 27-28 February 2004."

A press release issued by the International Union for Conservation of Nature (IUCN), dated September 2, 2009, "Last chance to save saola from extinction."

A press release issued by the International Union for Conservation of Nature (IUCN), dated May 21, 2012, "Saola still a mystery 20 years after its spectacular debut."

A report by Elizabeth Kemf, published by WWF—World Wide Fund for Nature (formerly World Wildlife Fund, which remains the organization's official name in Canada and the United States), dated August 2013, "The Saola's battle for survival on the Ho Chi Minh trail."

A book by William deBuys, published by Little, Brown in 2015, *The Last Unicorn: A Search for One of Earth's Rarest Creatures*.

A news article by Jason Bittel, published in the *Washington Post*, dated March 27, 2019, "Saving the 'Asian Unicorns': How do you protect what you can't see?"

A report by R. J. Timmins, S. Hedges, and W. Robichaud, published by the International Union for Conservation of Nature and Natural Resources, dated 2020, "*Pseudoryx nghetinhensis* (amended version of 2016 assessment), *The IUCN Red List of Threatened Species* 2020: e.T18597A166485696."

A report published by WWF-Greater Mekong, dated 2021, "New Species Discoveries in the Greater Mekong 2020."

A press release issued by the International Union for Conservation of Nature (IUCN), dated August 20, 2021, "IUCN SSC experts urge for immediate action to find Saola before it's too late."

A news article by Veronika Perková published in the *Guardian*, dated January 7, 2022, "Scientists step up hunt for 'Asian unicorn,' one of world's rarest animals."

A blog entry by William Robichaud, posted to the blog *A Bird in the Bush*, dated April 17, 2023, "Secret wars, secret creatures, and hope." (The entry was also posted in the newsletter of the *Saola Foundation* on April 17, 2023.)

The poem "Camera Trap Triptych" was inspired by the following sources:

William deBuys's book, *The Last Unicorn: A Search for One of Earth's Rarest Creatures*, which includes two photographs of wild saola caught on camera trap.

One photo that inspired this poem was taken in 1998 in Pu Mat National Park in Vietnam. The photo is credited to the European Commission, Social Forestry and Nature Conservation (SFNC)/Fauna & Flora International and can be found online at https://www.fauna-flora.org/news/discovery-channel-the-iconic-importance-of-new-species-in-an-age-of-biodiversity-loss/. It is an image of the first ever wild saola caught on a camera trap photo.

Another photo from deBuys's book was captured in 1999 in Ban Vangban village located in Bolikhamxay province, central Laos. The photo is credited to William Robichaud, Wildlife Conservation Society. This photo can also be found online on the IUCN website: https://iucn.org/news/species-survival-commission/202108/iucn-ssc-experts-urge-immediate-action-find-saola-its-too-late. The creation and design for the cover of this book was inspired by this image.

A third photo from deBuys's book shows a saola in the Central Annamite Mountains of Vietnam. It was taken on September 7, 2013, and released by WWF. The photo can also be found online on the WWF website: https://wwf.panda.org/wwf_news/?212298/Saola-rediscovered-Asian-Unicorn-sighted-in-Vietnam-for-first-time-in-15-years. This image represents the last public and known sighting of a saola caught on camera trap.

The poem "Hmong, An Ethnographic Study of Other" draws from the following source:

A scholarly article by Luang Boriphandh Dhuraratsadorn and translated by Erik Seidenfaden, published in Volume 17 (Issue 3) of *Journal of the Siam Society*, dated December 1923, "The White Meo."

The poem "Autonomous Sky" draws from the following sources:

A report published by the Unrepresented Nations and Peoples Organization, dated February 2017, "Briefing Note: Current Situation of Hmong People in Laos (2017)."

A report published by the Unrepresented Nations and Peoples Organization, dated July 2017, "Member Profile: Hmong, Congress of World Hmong People (CWHP)."

A report published by the Unrepresented Nations and Peoples Organization, dated March 20, 2018, "Midterm Universal Periodic Review on Laos."

A joint allegation letter to the government of the Lao People's Democratic Republic, from United Nations Special Rapporteurs, dated August 28, 2020, subject: "Information received concerning the alarming situation of the Hmong indigenous community located in the Phou Bia region (referred to as the 'ChaoFa Hmong'), including the indiscriminate attacks against the community, enforced and involuntary disappearances, denying access to food and lacking health care and access to safe and drinking water."

A report published by the Unrepresented Nations and Peoples Organization, dated April 2021, "Hmong in Isolation: Atrocities against the indigenous Hmong in the Xaisomboun Region of Laos."

A joint allegation follow-up letter to the government of the Lao People's Democratic Republic, from United Nations Special Rapporteurs, dated April 27, 2021, subject: "Information received concerning the situation of the Hmong community located in the Phou Bia region, referred as to 'ChaoFa Hmong'. More precisely, with regards to reported acts of intimidation and reprisals by the Lao military forces against the relatives of an elderly Hmong man and three Hmong girls, victims of enforced disappearance since March 2020, following an intervention by Special Procedures mandate-holders on 31 August 2020."

A letter from Mercè Monje Cano, Executive Director, Unrepresented Nations and Peoples Organization, to Michael Fakhri, Special Rapporteur on the Right to Food, and Ilze Brands Kehris, Assistant Secretary-General for Human Rights, Office of the United Nations High Commissioner for Human Rights (OHCHR), dated February 23, 2022, regarding: "Follow-up communication on the crisis facing the ChaoFa Hmong in the Lao People's Democratic Republic."

ACKNOWLEDGMENTS

With gratitude to the following journals where versions of these poems first appeared:

The Academy of American Poets' *Poem-a-Day*: "Out of Research into Reveries"
AGNI: "Chant of Immediate Threats" and "Node: When in the end"
Alta Journal: "Take to the Days a Fist of Starlight"
Narrative: "Tame External Features Come Birthing Endangered in a Cage"
The Nation: "Death in Captivity, a Surrender"
Poetry: "Look to the New Moon" and "I Understand This Light to Be My Home"
Prairie Schooner: "You Belong with the Waking" and "Injury after Another"
Shelter in Poems (poets.org): "In the Year of Permutations"

"Ars Poetica" and "Nocturne for the Bereft" appeared in *The Eloquent Poem: 128 Contemporary Poems and Their Making*, edited by Elise Paschen, published by Persea Books, 2019.

"That All, Everyone, Each in Being" appeared in 2020 as part of *Project 19*, a collaboration between the Academy of American Poets and the New York Philharmonic commemorating the centennial of the Ninteenth Amendment and featuring the work of nineteen women composers as well as nineteen women poets.

"Forest of Beginnings" appeared as part of Pao Houa Her's exhibition *Paj qaum ntuj / Flowers of the Sky* at the Walker Art Center and published at walkerart.org. The poem also appeared in Pao Houa Her's monograph *My grandfather turned into a tiger . . . and other illusions*, published by Aperture, 2024.

Huge thanks to William Robichaud for your decades of dedication to saola conservation and for taking time to chat with me. Thank you to William deBuys for your insight and conversation. Thanks also to Lorraine Scotson and everyone at the Saola Foundation for your continued advocacy in the field and elsewhere.

Gratitude to the Guggenheim Foundation and the College of Arts and Humanities at Fresno State. To my colleagues and students, thank you for the support and encouragement.

With appreciation to friends and mentors who continue to inspire and cheer me on: Cyrus Cassells, Carmen Giménez, Rigoberto González, Juan Felipe Herrera, Viet Thanh Nguyen, Monica Sok, Kao Kalia Yang, and Emily Yoon.

To Mei-mei Berssenbrugge whose words have been a source of light.

Cheers to everyone at Graywolf Press for all that you do and for bringing this book into existence. Big heartfelt thanks especially to editor Jeff Shotts—thank you for your guidance in shaping this collection and for simply believing in my work. My gratitude to Brittany Torres Rivera, Marisa Atkinson, Katie Dublinski, and the rest of the Graywolf team.

For your words in support of this book, for how your work has inspired me, it's my honor to thank you, Douglas Kearney and Hoa Nguyen.

To my father, to my mother—I write from a place inspired by you both, ua tsaug rau neb ob leeg pab kuv npau suav. To my siblings, Pa, Mary, Larly, Peg, Bob, Cindy, and Amy, along with Txiv laus Chuck, Txiv hluas Soua, Txiv hluas George, Txiv hluas Chee, Edward, and Eddie, as well as my delightful band of nieces and nephews, Leilani, Landon, Ryan, Carter, Matthew, Gwen, Charlotte, Dara, Wesley, Vincent, Madison, and Sophie, together with the Cody and Brown families—thank you all for surrounding me with your love, nourishment, and care.

To Anthony, ever-abiding and always you.

To Máximo Rafael-Muajhmoov Cody, may you grow to love this earth just as much and more. All the more for you.

To learn more about saola conservation or support efforts
to save species on the brink of extinction in Southeast Asia,
please visit the following resources:

The Saola Foundation
saolafoundation.org

Asian Species Action Partnership
speciesonthebrink.org

MAI DER VANG is the author of *Yellow Rain*, winner of the Lenore Marshall Poetry Prize from the Academy of American Poets, an American Book Award, and a Northern California Book Award. *Yellow Rain* was also a finalist for the Pulitzer Prize in Poetry, the PEN/Voelcker Award, the Los Angeles Times Book Prize, and the California Book Award. Her first book, *Afterland*, received the First Book Award from the Academy of American Poets, was longlisted for the National Book Award, and was a finalist for the Kate Tufts Discovery Award. The recipient of a Guggenheim Fellowship and a Lannan Literary Fellowship, she teaches in the MFA program in creative writing at Fresno State.

Graywolf Press publishes risk-taking, visionary writers who transform culture through literature. As a nonprofit organization, Graywolf relies on the generous support of its donors to bring books like this one into the world.

This publication is made possible, in part, by the voters of Minnesota through a Minnesota State Arts Board Operating Support grant, thanks to a legislative appropriation from the arts and cultural heritage fund. Significant support has also been provided by other generous contributions from foundations, corporations, and individuals. To these supporters we offer our heartfelt thanks.

To learn more about Graywolf's books and authors
or make a tax-deductible donation, please visit
www.graywolfpress.org.

The text of *Primordial* is set in Adobe Caslon Pro.
Book design by Rachel Holscher.
Composition by Bookmobile Design & Digital
Publisher Services, Minneapolis, Minnesota.
Manufactured by Sheridan on acid-free,
30 percent postconsumer wastepaper.